UNIFORMS

UNIFORMS

❖

David G. Duchesneau

To order additional copies of this book, contact:
Xlibris LLC
1-888-795-4274
www.Xlibris.com
Orders@Xlibris.com
540873

CONTENTS

Dedication

This book is in memory of my Mom
Angele Renda (Ferland) Duchesneau
who has always been there with her love
and strength and understanding.

ACKNOWLEDGEMENTS

Through the course of my early years of life, attending Parochial School, being a member of the Graniteers Drum and Bugle Corps and through my Marine Corps years in Boot Camp and serving two tours of Duty in Vietnam, I had the good fortune to meet and come into contact with several hundreds, if not thousands, of people. Their memories, along with their actions and comments, contributed to this book. Without them, this book would not have been possible.

Special thanks is extended to my lifelong friend, Raymond Turmelle, for all his help and support that he has given me throughout the years and his continued guidance in supplying photographs for this project.

To Stephen, for his computer expertise with generating scanned images for the manuscript.

To Andrea, for all of her hard work and support and believing in me, and for all of the arduous hours she has spent in editing my manuscript.

I am further indebted to Xlibris, my Publishing Team, for all their patience and guidance which separates written manuscripts from published books.

To all of these people who have made my dream come true, transforming my manuscript, *UNIFORMS,* into a book. Thank you!

INTRODUCTION

This book, *Uniforms*, spans an era in a boy's life that tells about his experiences growing up in a small New England town, from his childhood years, attending parochial school, to his adolescent years, continuing parochial school and becoming an active member of a drum and bugle corps for ten years. The story continues into early adulthood when he enlisted into the United States Marine Corps, through boot camp, and then serving two tours of duty, 1969 through 1970, in Vietnam.

It is a factual description of his life as he grew up and through his experiences of wearing many *uniforms*, which shaped his life and future forever.

The language used in this book is sometimes graphic, with four-letter expressions. However, it is the exact language that was so commonly used during that era.

The author does his best at explaining what it was like to grow up in the late 1950s and the 1960s, attending school taught only by nuns. Then while still attending school, joining a drum and bugle corps and all his experiences traveling around New England and Canada, performing in parades and field competitions. At eighteen years old, he enlisted into the Armed Forces, United States Marine Corps, and explains what life was like at eighteen years old in 1968 to go through boot camp at Parris Island in South Carolina. As his marine infantry training continued, the author describes, in detail and in his own words, what it was like as the Marine Corps prepared him and many others like him for combat in Vietnam. The author then describes, to the best of his recollection and ability, what life was like in Vietnam in 1969 while he was attached to a marine combat unit in Quang Tri Province of Southern Vietnam. The book goes on to describe how, at the end of 1969, he was redeployed to another combat unit south of Da Nang. The author stayed in Vietnam until mid-August of 1970 and then was released from active duty and returned home at the age of twenty-one.

This book speaks from the heart and mind of everyone who has ever had the experience of attending a Catholic school with nuns, all those who were ever so fortunate to be a member of a drum and bugle corps, and all those combat veterans who served in Vietnam and experienced the rigors and sorrows of that war.

CHAPTER 1

Childhood

The Early Years

It all started a long time ago. As you get older, you finally realize that you have no say at all where you came from. I guess it's just the pick of the draw. You're born and your parents and siblings are what you have, and that's it. God stuck you with them and them with you. You try and make the best of what God gave you. That's how simple life really is.

I was a kid who grew up in a small northern New England town. Things were really simple back then. Either your parents had money or they didn't. There was no so-called middle class. We lived in a home where our parents didn't have much money. Our parents struggled, and we seemed to have just enough to get by. But we didn't know any difference anyway. The whole neighborhood was just the same as we were. Yes, some families may have had a newer car or a bigger house, but we had the only color TV on the block, and all our friends would hang out at our house so that they could watch our TV, especially kid shows like the *Howdy Doody Show*.

Our father, who was a firefighter, was a hard man. He worked all the time and, for some reason, just could not get ahead. He always felt and acted like life shortchanged him, and he was always angry at something. He had a disposition like a polar bear, sitting his ass on a cold piece of ice, and just couldn't get himself to warm up at all. He was a miserable person, and he didn't like too many people. Hell, I don't think he even liked us much either. It seemed like life really sucked for him and that he felt sorry for the life that God dealt him.

When he wasn't working at the fire department and was on his days off, he did electrical work on the side, just to have enough money to get by. And let me tell you, was he tight with his money. I bet that he always had his first nickel he ever made. He was tighter with his money than bark on a tree. Now get this right, he wasn't a frugal person or anything; he was just a tightwad. We never dared ask him for a dime. Once, I asked him for fifty cents, and one would think that I had asked him for his last buck. I think it had to do with school or something, but I remember making the mistake of asking him while we were eating at the dinner table. The old man got so angry, and when he got angry, he started to shake and his face got red. He reached quickly into his pocket and took out fifty cents, threw a punch just past my nose, and put a big hole in the wall. Then he threw that fifty-cent coin right at me. Well, what do you think? Do you think that it cost him more than fifty cents to fix that damn hole in the wall than just to give me the fifty cents?

Back to doing electrical work on the side. Now that was a great time. He would either take my older brother or me to work with him. Most of the time it was me, because my brother was older and hated going to work with Dad. He would make himself scarce, plus he had a paper route. Well, let me tell you, did I hate that. I'd go with him as his helper, his gofer. He would be doing something with electrical wires, and he would look at me and say, "Go in the trunk and get the what's-a-call-it." Well, let me tell you this, at six or seven years old, everything in that trunk was a "what's-a-call-it." How the hell did I know what he wanted? So I would ask him what he meant, what exactly was the tool that he wanted me to get from the trunk? So he'd say, "You know what I mean, the thingamajig." And then I'd get that famous saying "Jesus Christ, do I have to hit you over the head with a crowbar?" or "Do I have to hit you with a two-by-four?" Well, that was stupid. What did he think? Yes, Dad, hit me over the head with either that two-by-four or the crowbar. That will surely smarten me up for next time. Going to work with him was a real treat. The old man was a real charmer, full of love and compassion. Yeah, right!

Our mother, on the other hand, was a saint and had to put up with everything that Dad dished out. She taught us to respect him, and we did respect him—well, kind of, because we actually respected him out of fear. Mom really tried hard to keep the family together and as happy as she could. One day, I talked my mom into letting me get a pet duck—yes, a duck—for Easter. It was a little yellow duck that she bought for me at the local five-and-dime store, Woolworths. Well, I had this baby duck in a box in the basement, and I had to keep him warm, so I put a light bulb on an extension cord above him in the box. Well, Mom knew that my dad was a stickler about keeping lights on, so when I went to bed, Mom went down in the basement to check on the duck, and she shut the light off. Hell, she didn't want to piss off the old man. Well, my little duck got cold and froze. I got up in the morning and went to check on my duck. He wasn't moving at all. I saw that the light was off, and I guess I started crying. My mom came down into the basement to see why I was crying, and she saw that the duck was dead. I can tell you that Mom felt so bad. She kept apologizing to me and held me tight and told me that she was so sorry. Well, the duck was dead, the light was off, and Dad wasn't angry about having a light on all night.

Dad would yell and swear at us. Hell, at one point, I didn't know if my name was Jesus Christ or goddamn it. It was always something like "Goddamn it, don't you know better?" or "Jesus Christ, why did you do that?" The only good thing about him being a firefighter was that his work schedule would be twenty-four-hour shifts. So we at least had a break and only had to deal with him every other day or so, but we did have Mom. That was rough at times too, because when we would act up like most kids do, Mom would just say things like "Wait until your father gets home." And the one saying I always loved was "When your father gets home, you guys are going to know it." Yes, well, no shit! I would always think to myself, *Of course we're going to know it.* Dad was always after us. We couldn't do anything right at all. He found fault with everything. And when he'd get worked up or when we would piss him off, which was about every day, he would chase us around, trying to catch us, and he'd love to kick you square in the ass. Hell, I cannot tell you how many times I'd come into the house and Dad's foot would be right on my ass, as I'd try and run past him upstairs to my room. One time Dad broke his leg while doing electrical work. I guess that he was on a ladder or something, God only knows, and somehow, he fell off the ladder and landed in the basement on the concrete floor of the new house that he was wiring. Anyway, there he was, leg in a full cast and on crutches. Shit, he was home all the time, and when he'd get angry at me, he would chase me around the yard, trying to catch me so that he could get that good foot of his up my ass. It was kind of funny to see him trying to run with one foot and two crutches. Hell, he looked like old man McCoy of the TV show *The Real McCoys*. After a while, he got good at using his crutches to run around. As I got older, it got to be a joke, because I was the tallest one in the family, and the joke was that I was tall because Dad always kicked me in the ass, and it made me taller than any of my brothers or sisters. Some joke! I always said to myself that I'd rather have him kick me than get hit by that freaking black belt he wore. At least I got one kick at a time, where the belt was ongoing for at least five or six hits. Like I said, the old man was a real charmer. You know, he always figured that he made nothing of himself out of his life. He always wanted to go to school, but he couldn't because he didn't have the money. Shit, one time he was talking about moving us all to Australia. Now, what in hell ever made him think that his life would be better off by moving to another country? That would have been real smart. I guess he liked Australia, because while Dad was in the marines during World War II, he went on leave once to Australia. I can only imagine that he met some girl, and for all we know, we might have a brother or sister out there. Who knows? Anyway, we never did move.

Life as a preschooler was great fun in our house. You know, I loved my dad. After all, he was my dad, and I couldn't do anything about that, but I sure as hell did not like him, and I think he felt the same about me. He loved me even though he never told me that he loved me, not once. If the truth be known, if he wasn't my dad and I wasn't his son, I know that we would not have had anything at all to do with one another. He was a real bastard. One time though, my mom got very angry at us. She rarely got very angry, but this day she did. You see, my brother, my cousin, and I all went down the road to this pond. This pond was always there. It was like a big sandpit, which was now full of water. We used to ice-skate on it during the winter. Well, on this summer day, we went to the pond. We called it the frog pond, and we found a raft that was strung together with rope. There was a homemade paddle, and my brother, my cousin, and I decided that it would be fun to take the raft out. So we did. Well, one thing led to another, and we all started arguing about who was going to use the paddle. Well, the paddle went flying into the water. Here we sat, in the middle of this pond, on this raft, with no paddle. You know, like up the creek without a paddle. That was us! My cousin panicked and decided to jump in and swim to shore. Well, he did jump into the water, clothes and all. Then, all of a sudden, he must have gotten caught in some underwater brush or something, and he started to go underwater. I jumped in and tried to save him. My brother kept yelling at me to swim on my back, so I did. I reached my cousin and tried to help him, but he kept pulling me underwater. He started to panic and just kept pulling me under. My brother was yelling at me to get away from him and to swim on my back. The next thing I knew, my brother jumped into the water and tried to get my cousin, but again, all my cousin did was pull my brother underwater. My brother finally kicked away from my cousin, and the next thing I knew, this teenage boy came out of nowhere, grabbed me, and pulled me out of the water and up on the dirt bank. This teenager then swam out and saved my cousin from drowning and pulled him up on the side of the bank. The next thing I knew, my cousin and I were being loaded up into an ambulance. Who the hell called for an ambulance anyway? Well, we were rushed to the hospital and into the emergency room. I had no idea where my brother was, but I knew he wasn't with us. Anyway, they checked us out, and we were OK. The next thing I remember was seeing my dad. The old man did not say a word. After a while, we got released, and my dad took me home. Well, let me tell you, I never saw my mom so angry. She was yelling and screaming, and she kept hitting me in the face and slapping me on the side of my head and told me to go to my room and not move. I guess that Mom was so scared at what could have happened to us, drowning or something like that. She just lost it. This was the first and last time I saw Mom so angry, and Dad never said a word or did anything. He just stood there and watched as my mom was hitting and slapping me. I will never forget that day as long as I live.

CHAPTER 2

Parochial School

Being from a French Catholic family, we went to a Catholic school and had Holy Cross nuns for teachers. This would be my first of many uniforms that I was to wear during my life. Boys at this school were dressed in slacks, white shirts, and blue blazers. Girls were in blue skirts and white blouses. Well, let me tell you, these sisters were tough. They did not put up with anything at all. They had no sense of humor. I think these nuns were probably trained by sadistic hoodlums or by the Nazis. They probably all served in Hitler's private secret police. They had their own ideas of what was right, and their punishment techniques were very unusual. Actually, they were not human. All I know is that the nuns were really mean. If you talked out of turn, they would come up and slap your face or hit you with either a pointer or a wooden ruler, or they would pick you up by taking these wooden clappers and pulling you up by your ear. I remember my first day at school. I was in the lunch line in the cafeteria, and I saw my older brother in line, waiting to get his food. I walked up to my brother and asked him what we were supposed to do, and this big nun, who looked like a big penguin, marched over to me, slapped me right in the face, grabbed me by the ear, and marched me away to the back of the lunch line. Well, how's that for an impression of how your school years are going to go?

That was my first day. I got home and told my mom and dad about the nun hitting me, and the old man said, "Well, you must have deserved it. Nuns just don't hit you for nothing." Yeah right, no pity from him. Mom just looked and said nothing. As far as Dad was concerned, the nuns were never wrong. For God's sake, they are nuns. They would never lie or stretch the truth. Yeah, bullshit. These nuns really sucked.

School just seemed to get worse and worse. We had French all
morning and English in the afternoon. I couldn't wait for recess. That
was really something—the girls on one side of the school yard and the
boys on the other side, with nuns patrolling the center. Heaven forbid
if you try going on the girls' side. Those nuns would be on you like
shingles on a roof. On the boys' side of the yard, there was this big
iron jungle gym, and on the girls' side, there were swings. One day,
I was running in the play yard. It was all hot-top (asphalt) and I ran
through a puddle. Well, I didn't mean to splash anyone, but an older
boy—eighth grader—got splashed, and his trousers got wet. He got so
angry that he came over to me and kicked me right in the balls. I was a
first grader! What do you think? I was rolling around on the pavement,
crying and hanging onto my crotch. A nun came over, grabbed me by
the hair, lifted me off the ground, and marched me into the principal's
office. I was crying all the way and trying to walk as best as I could.
The principal scolded me and told me that she was going to call the
parish pastor and that the pastor would call my father. What do you
think? The pastor came over, and he's a grumpy old priest, and all the
while, he's talking French. Hell, like I said, "I'm a first grade kid." I
don't have any clue what in hell he's saying. All I know was that some
eighth grader kicked me in the nuts and I'm in trouble. Go figure.
After school, the nuns made me stay and write stuff on the blackboard.
After writing, they made me clean all the blackboards and wash the
floors. Remember, I'm in first grade! Finally, the nuns let me out, and
I went home. I was walking home, alone, trying to figure out what the
hell my father was going to say. I got home, and of course, I was late.
I walked into the house, and it's almost time for supper. I sat down at
the table; my place was right next to my dad. Did I hate that! My older
sister sat across from me, and my brother sat to the right of me, next
to my mom. He knew enough not to sit next to the old man. Anyway,
I sat down, and all of a sudden I hear, "What did you do today? How
was school?" I looked at my mom and then at my dad and told him
what happened in the school yard. How do you think that went? Of
course it was my fault—I was running. God, who ever heard of a kid
running in a playground? What the hell was I thinking? Can't I just
be good? My father got so worked up that he was shaking. So I got a
good slap on the side of my head from him and I started crying, and
then he informed me that if I kept on crying, he was going to really
give me something to cry about. That's all I needed to hear. Boy, did

I love school! I dreaded each day. And we walked back and forth to school every day, rain or shine. Many days it did rain, and we would show up completely drenched. But that was all right. And during the winter, we had on these big boots and clumsy coats. But we walked every day, about two miles to and from school. As my father always said, it was good for us to walk. Dinnertime was always a real good time, especially if my dad cooked. He made these stupid meals, like eggs and spinach, blood sausage, which we called horse cock, or liver and onions. Hey, we were kids, who the hell eats this shit? And if you didn't eat it, then you didn't eat at all. He would just yell at us and tell us to go to our room. I can remember one time my sister was humming while at the dinner table. The old man must have told her three or four times to stop humming at the table. Well, she did not stop fast enough for him, so there he went. He slapped her on the side of the head and told her, "I told you to stop humming, now stop humming or you'll get another one." Way to go, Dad. I told you that he was a real charmer to be around.

Now, like I said, my brother and sister were older, and I always tried to hang around with my brother. After all, he was my older brother, and you would think that he would kind of take care of me. Don't get me wrong; once in a while he did watch over me and wouldn't let any of his friends or the older kids hurt me, but I always got those famous words, "Hey, you're too small to be hanging around with us." So I always tried to act older than I really was so that he and his friends would accept me. Sometimes it worked and sometimes it didn't.

Second grade didn't seem to get any better—French classes in the morning and English in the afternoon. My grades were not really that good, and I dreaded when report cards came out. I remember trying to hide the report card from my father because I knew that I was going to get his wrath. My brother was two years older than me, and my sister was two years older than my brother. We all got our report cards on the same day. My sister was always an honor student, and she could not wait to show her report card to our parents. So they always knew when we had our report cards, and Mom would ask to see it. My brother and I just barely got by, and we would hear it from Dad about how stupid we were and why weren't we more like our sister? Even the nuns would say that we should be more like our older sister. Let me tell you, it was not easy being the youngest and following in school after an older sister who was always studying and doing homework. Hell,

I hardly understood anything the French teachers were saying. I was a kid! All I wanted was to be left alone and play with my friends. I wanted to do kid things, that's all. Of course, our kid things were very different than they are today. I didn't own a bike, never even saw a skateboard. No iPod, computers, hell, we couldn't afford to go snow skiing or even sledding, so we used to hang on to the back of the milk truck and slide down the street while hanging onto the bumper of that truck. Then we would go ice-skating. I have no idea where those skates came from, but we did have them.

One day, my brother and I went skating at the frog pond. While I was skating, I saw this area of white foam. Now I had no idea that there was no ice under the foam. Yes, I skated through the foam and fell right into the water. I did everything I could do to get myself out of the water and back onto the ice. I finally got onto the ice, and now I was soaking wet. All I could think of was what my parents were going to say to me. I walked home, and luckily, no one was home. I quickly went to my room and changed up, but I left my wet clothes on the floor. Mom got home and found my wet clothes. I told my mom what happened, and to my surprise, she only told me to be more careful while I was skating and never to skate alone. I thought surely that I was going to catch hell, but I didn't. Apparently, what had happened was someone must have thrown some type of hazardous material into the water and it never froze. That damn frog pond was going to be the death of me yet!

We lived right across the street from the fairgrounds, and that was, in itself, very entertaining. My brother and I would care for the racehorses. These were the sulky-type horses. We would help the owners train the horses, clean the stalls, feed and bathe the horses—basically, do whatever the owners wanted us to do for their horses. We did this for fifty cents a day. One owner had a beautiful black stallion named Epic, and I worked for him for quite some time. The owner also had a pony and a female German shepherd named Queenie. I was able to ride that pony anytime I wanted, and the dog would follow me everywhere. I was even given permission to take Queenie and ride the pony home. I loved that dog, especially since I did not have a dog of my own yet. Dad hated dogs, or maybe, dogs hated Dad. Who knows? You know what they say about animals? They instinctively know who the good and kind people are. I guess they knew that Dad was just a mean, grumpy old bastard!

Anyway, the fair came every September for two weeks, and things got to be really exciting. I would get as many old rags together that I could and would trade the rags to the carnies, who set up and worked the rides, for free-ride tickets. I would save up every old piece of cloth all year long so that I could give them to the carnies. I never paid to go on any of the rides, and good thing because we had no money for rides. If I could have found a way, I think I would have taken the sheets off our beds and cut them up into rags so that I could have gotten more ride tickets, but I knew if I ever did that, my mom and dad would have really punished me. Hell, we had just enough money to be fed. The fair was huge. They had all kinds of rides, all kinds of games, horse races, and fun houses and even a girly show tent. One night during the fair, I remember sneaking a look under the girly show tent. I could not believe my eyes, as these girls were taking their clothes off, and the men were all yelling and clapping and throwing money at these girls as they took their clothes off. I don't think I'll ever forget that, and there was this smell inside that tent that I will never forget. It was like a kind of body odor that I never experienced before. I guess that these girls were not clean. I don't know. All I know is that it was a different smell I never experienced before.

Another time, one of the horse owners had this big ostrich as a pet for his horse. I remember the owner giving me this big ostrich egg, and I brought it home. Mom looked at me and asked where I got such a big egg and what I was going to do with that egg. Well, I showed her. I cracked the egg open and cooked scrambled eggs. There was enough from that one egg to feed all of us. Now that was kind of cool. I also learned that

I liked to cook. So anytime that my dad was working, I asked my mom if I could make supper, and I would make us all cheeseburgers. To me, it was a hell of a lot better than that shit my dad cooked. Now don't get me wrong; Mom was a good cook, but she worked, and she was tired. Plus, we always ate the same old things. Monday was leftover night, Tuesday was some kind of casserole night, Wednesday was spaghetti night, Thursday—who the hell knows, and Friday was tuna casserole. Saturday was hotdogs and beans, and Sunday was some kind of roast. So when I made cheeseburgers, it was a real treat for all of us.

I finally convinced my mom that we needed a dog of our own. We always had cats around, and we needed a dog. I knew that she felt so badly about killing my duck. I promised her that I would take good care of the dog, and I don't know how, but she talked to Dad, and the next thing I knew, we had a handsome brown-and-white beagle puppy. He was all mine and mine alone, and I named him Prince. I did everything with Prince. He even slept in my bed. He was my best friend ever. I took him everywhere. During the summertime, Dad would pack us all up, including Prince, and we would all go camping. Well, that was a lot of fun. Right! All of us sleeping in one tent—my mom and my dad, my sister, my brother, and me on the ground in sleeping bags. Even Prince slept with me in my sleeping bag. Dad would put newspapers on the tent floor, and we would sleep on these newspapers. One time it rained so hard that we got totally soaked. But that was all right, because we were on vacation, camping, and having fun. Then Dad would want to go hiking, and again, what a lot of fun that was. Heaven forbid if Dad took a wrong turn, which he did so often, and we would get lost. It was always either my mom or one of us, even sometimes the dog, that made him take that wrong turn and get us lost. But eventually, we would find our way back to the main road and hike back to our campsite. I remember during one of these wonderful hikes, we got so lost and it became late. We finally found our way back to the main road, about five miles from the campground. Well, my dad was hungry, so he decided to stop at this roadside restaurant. There was this big discussion about the dog and why did we have to have a dog anyway, but David wanted a dog and all, and what were we going to do with him while we ate. Well, guess what? I was told that the dog was mine and so it was my responsibility to stay outside with Prince while my mom, my dad, my brother, and my sister ate. So they all went inside the restaurant, and I sat outside with

Prince. About an hour later, or it may have been even longer—I know that it really seemed like a long time—they all came out, and I got a piece of bread or something like that. Prince was my dog; I wouldn't give him up for anything, and I gave him some of my bread.

It was my job to make sure that we had wood for the campfire. Prince and I would go out and knock down dead trees and break them up and bring them back to our campsite. I liked using the handheld ax to cut up the wood. I liked being out alone in the woods with Prince. I didn't have to worry about what I was doing or what Dad was going to say. It was just me and my dog and I loved it. Now remember, we didn't have much money, so I never owned a pair of sneakers. All I ever wore were penny loafers. Now just picture this—going camping, hiking, working in the fairgrounds with the horses, cleaning out the stalls, and shoveling horse manure with loafers on, and all the time, I never owned a pair of boots or sneakers. I always wore those loafers. And do you think we had money for a pair of blue jeans? Hell, no. I didn't even know what blue jeans were. I wore slacks all the time. No shorts, no jeans, no other pants other than slacks, and most of them were hand-me-downs from my older brother. And heaven forbid if I ever tore a hole in my slacks or if the soles of my shoes wore off. If I did, I had to put either paper or something in my shoes. Man, life was good! I couldn't even get a new pair of shoes if my life depended on it. Of course, sliding on the back of that milk truck didn't do any good for the soles of my shoes, but that didn't matter to me anyway. Hell, I was just a kid trying to have fun any way that I could.

On one of our camping trips, Dad came home from the fire station and packed us up quickly because he wanted to get going, and we drove way up to the White Mountains. We drove for what seemed like hours. Once at the campground, we started unpacking and setting up our camping area, and then it was time to put the tent up. Guess what happened? No poles for the tent. We forgot the tent poles at home. Of course, it was everyone else's fault other than my dad's. Man, was he pissed off. He was yelling, screaming, and telling us how stupid we all were and he was shouting "Jesus Christ" and "Goddamn it" everywhere. Then the old man looked at me and told me to get into the car, that we were going to drive back home to get the tent poles. You know, I just said to myself, "Oh good, Dad and me alone in the car." What a great treat. I was going to be alone with that bastard! God, I only thought, *Why me?* He told Mom, my brother, and my sister to set up everything else while we were gone. What a long ride back home and then a longer ride back to the campground. Dad never talked, and once in a while, he would just mumble something to himself. You know, it always seemed that Murphy's law was always with us. If it could happen to us, it did and it would. We drove into the campground just in time to see fire trucks and forest wardens all about our campsite and people everywhere. What happened was that my brother decided he would help my mom and start a campfire. Well, he couldn't get the fire started, so he took some gasoline from a can of gas that we had and started the fire. You can just figure out what happened next. The fire started all right, with an explosion! The gas can caught on fire, and my brother burned out our campsite. I guess that Prince was tied to the picnic table, and I guess he just escaped with his life. All his whiskers were burned off, and my brother singed both of his eyebrows. The tarp that was over the picnic table was all burned up. Our chuck box that Dad made, and all the food in it, was burned out. The entire site was charred. You should have seen the old man's face. This was the first time that I saw my dad speechless. He just walked around and looked around in amazement—or was it bewilderment? I never forgot that look on his face. It was like someone just beat the shit out of him. He wanted to just pack up what he could salvage and leave. But with help from other families who were also camping, they talked to Dad, and we were given enough camping gear to stay. We even drove into a nearby town and bought a new tent. After that, the old man appeared to calm down for the remainder of our camping vacation. He was like a beaten man, and he was very quiet. Like I said, vacations were just a joy. We never knew what the old man was going to get us into. I really got to hate vacations and those stupid camping trips.

Once back home, we still had more than a month before summer ended and school started. I kept playing in the fairgrounds with my dog. The old man could not just let us hang around all day, so he brought us to our uncle's farm. Now, that was another real treat from the old man. During the daytime, we would help out by haying the fields. This was fun trying to pick up those bales of hay and throwing them on the back of this old red flatbed truck. Hell, I could just barely get the bales of hay off the ground and onto the back of that truck. After all, I was just a small kid. The only good thing is that, once in a while, I was able to drive that stupid old red truck. Yes, every once in a while, I would get in the truck, which had a stick shift, and I actually learned how to drive that truck. I taught myself how to use a stick shift. Now let me tell you, I could just barely reach the pedals, and could I grind those gears. Now, that was fun! I'd drive around the field, and no one said a word. Once in a while, if it rained and we could not do the haying, we would play in the barn. One day, my cousin and I went to the bull barn. Let me tell you, these bulls were big and mean. We would work up the bulls by poking them with a pitchfork. One day we worked up this bull so much that my uncle walked over to see what was causing the bulls to act up. My uncle tried to calm the bulls down, and somehow, one of the bulls horned my uncle right in his thigh. Man, was my uncle pissed at us. Needless to say, we were banned from ever going into the bull barn again.

At night, we would stay at my grandparents' house. Now, that was a story in itself. These were my dad's parents, and his mother—my grandmother—had no sense of humor at all. Now I know where my dad got his mean streak from—her! She didn't like me, and I didn't like her. She was a really mean woman, and now I know why my father was the way he was. One day, for whatever reason, I didn't go to the farm with my grandfather. So I was left with my grandmother, and the next thing I know, she took me by the arm and locked me in the basement. Now here I was, seven or eight years old, and this crazy woman locked me in the basement. The basement had a dirt floor and spiderwebs everywhere. There was one stupid light on in the entire basement. I didn't dare move from the bottom step. I sat on that bottom step and imagined all kinds of things, like gigantic bugs and spiders, were going to get me. Then there was this copper-colored contraption that was making some type of clear liquid. Little did I know that this was my grandfather's still. Yes, my grandfather made his own moonshine. That thing was scary looking, with its copper coils and all. I stayed there in the basement for what seemed forever, and finally, I heard the door open, and my grandfather came down to get me. After that, I begged my mother not to leave me with my grandparents, and of course, my dad thought that I was not telling the truth because his mother would never do that. Right, Dad, way to go! I made it all up. Sure I did.

Summer was over before you knew it, and it was time to go back to school. Mom went to work, we went back to school, and Prince stayed home alone. Third grade started, and it seemed that things were not getting any better. I still could not understand the French teachers, and I was having a hard time concentrating on anything. We had this one teacher by the name of Sister Saint Josepha, and we called her Josefat. I thought to myself, who named these nuns anyway? They were far from being saints so why did they get to be named Sister Saint anything? Every time her back was to us and she would be writing on the blackboard, I would throw something at her. One day I took a blackboard eraser that was full of white chalk, and I threw it at her. She had this big white spot on the back of her black gown. Was she ever pissed off, and she tried to get one of the girls in our class to tell her who threw the eraser, but nobody told on me. Then we had another nun by the name of Sister Saint Paul. Some saint she was. She was one of the French teachers, and she only spoke French. Now, she was a real prize. One day she heard some boys swearing in the school yard, and after recess, she took all the boys and asked us, in French, who was swearing and saying things like *hell, shit, goddamn*, and *Jesus Christ*, but nobody said a word. Third grade really sucked. If you really got in trouble and you were bad, the nuns would make you stay after school and wash their floors. The nuns' living quarters were adjacent to the school. They would give us a pail of soapy water, and we were made to wash their bedroom floors. I remember hearing stories about the nuns getting boys into their rooms and making the boys take their pants down so that the nun could slap their butts. Now, what in hell was that all about anyway? Why would these nuns make a kid take his pants down? I told you earlier that these nuns were really mean, and it was like they had training for torture techniques. Shit, if they could have, I bet they would have waterboarded us. Who knows?

Prince and I would still go into the woods around the fairgrounds. We had a ball playing army and going by a small brook that was behind the fairgrounds. One day, I came home from school and couldn't find Prince. I didn't know where he was. I looked all over the house and neighborhood, but Prince was nowhere to be found. When my mom got home, I asked her if she knew where Prince was. She didn't say a word, and I kept looking for him all over the place. I went into the fairgrounds and into the woods, calling his name. I couldn't find my dog anywhere. I guess I was so bad, and I kept crying because my dog was not around. After about a week, my mom took me aside and told me that Dad had taken Prince away. I was crying so hard and asked where he took him. Mom said that a neighbor approached Dad and said that Prince nipped at her. I knew my dog, and he wouldn't bite or nip anybody unless that person tried to hurt him. Anyway, I kept asking Mom where Dad took my dog, and she just said that he was gone and that he wasn't coming back. I approached my dad. I was crying, and I asked him, point-blank, what he did to Prince. He got excited and started shaking and said that Prince was a bad dog and attacked a neighbor. I told him that Prince would never do that, but he insisted that he did. I asked him who told him, who complained about Prince, and he finally told me that it was an older lady down the street. I approached that lady, but she wouldn't talk to me. I kept calling her a dog killer, and finally, she came to our house and asked my mom and dad if they could get me to stop calling her a dog killer. I guess that I was after her so much and yelling at her each time I passed by her house that she was having a breakdown. Anyway, my father had Prince put to sleep. I never did forgive him for that. It was another typical thing that this mean bastard did to me. After a while, I kind of lightened up, and all I did was remember the good times that I shared with my dog. Time has a way of healing bad things.

As I started getting older, into puberty—I had no idea what puberty was—the one thing I did start being curious about were the girls. I started noticing the girls in my classes, and I liked it. I figured out that girls talked softly, that they smelled good, and if you got a chance to hold their hands, that their hands were nice and soft. All I wanted to do was to talk with them and be around them. I wanted to walk to school with them. I wanted to hold their hands. I just wanted to be near them. We had this hangout, a restaurant right across the street from our school, and we would go there after school. It would be filled with girls, and we would drink Coca-Cola and have french fries. Good thing that I worked in the fairgrounds for those horsemen. At least I had a little money to pay for an occasional Coke and fries. Heaven forbid if I had to ask Dad for any money. Remember, like I said earlier, I once asked Dad for fifty cents. Holy shit, you think I asked him for a hundred bucks. He got so angry at me that he put his fist through a wall in our kitchen. Heaven forbid that I had the nerve to ask him for any money. I thought to myself, *I wonder how much it cost him to fix that wall?* I'll bet you it was more than fifty cents. Who knows? I never asked him for any money, or anything, after that.

CHAPTER 3

Drum and Bugle Corps

1958-1968

Dad thought that we needed something more, because all we did was hang around in the fairgrounds. He thought that we might get ourselves in trouble because kids were always causing damage and breaking into the different buildings. So when I was eight years old, Dad enrolled my older brother, sister, and me into a drum and bugle corps. This was the second uniform that I was to wear. Let's get something straight right from the beginning. A drum and bugle corps is not a band. As a matter of fact, it's far from anything that a band is. A drum and bugle corps is just what it says—drums and bugles. No trumpets, trombones, saxophones, clarinets, or any reed instruments other than just drums, bugles, and a color guard. We had nothing to do with any schools or bands. The kids in the corps were not nerds, and most of us were tough street kids, and some of us were wise guys. Hell, we had kids that would get into trouble, get picked up by the police, and go to juvenile court. The judge of that juvenile court knew the corps director really well, and the judge would make a deal with many of these kids; they could either serve time in a juvenile-detention center in Manchester or join the drum corps instead. So we had several juvenile offenders in the corps. And for the most part, they were good guys. They just came from broken homes, or their parent's didn't want anything to do with them and they needed something better in their lives. The corps gave them that.

Now let's get back to when Dad brought us to join. I remember that night that he carted us down there. I saw all these kids and people I never knew, and of course, Dad said it would be good for us. I think Dad meant that it would be good for him. My brother was bullshit. He wanted to play little league baseball. No, Dad wanted us to be in the corps. I was the youngest member to join that night. Again, I was at least two years younger than most of the kids, and it was hard for me to fit in with them. Hell, they didn't want any kid younger than them trying to hang around, but I did fit in because they quickly learned that I liked to smoke cigarettes, I swore like a parrot, and I always tried to act like a wise guy. Hell, I even got my brother hooked on smoking. I used to steal cigarettes from my mom's pack; she smoked Pall Mall cigarettes, and I would share the smoke with my brother. Anyway, I did fit in the best I could. The minimum age to join the corps was supposed to be at least ten years old, but somehow, the old man talked the corps director into letting me join. I asked if I could play drums. They put me in the drum section, and I quickly learned that playing drums was not as easy as it looked. Anyway, I wasn't any good at drums; I had no hand coordination at all, so they put me in the horn section. Now let me tell you, I didn't know one end of the horn—a bugle—from the other. I never played a bugle, and I couldn't read music. Shit, I had all I could do to just read English and French, never mind music, but Dad figured that this would keep us out of trouble and off the streets. Well, guess what? The drum corps kept us on the streets—all the main streets in the state. Every weekend, we would be out there parading. Then as the corps grew and we got better, we started to perform in drum corps contests. Talk about being busy. During the week, we would practice in the evenings until ten o'clock. On weekends and holidays, we would be out there in some town in New England, doing our thing, marching and playing. They scheduled parades every chance the corps got. We even paraded for John F. Kennedy, and every time that Kennedy came to New Hampshire, he would ask the corps to play and march for his presidential election campaign. I even got to meet him and shake his hand. Kennedy did win the 1960 presidential election, and the corps was selected to represent the state at his inauguration, so we even got to march in Washington, DC, on Pennsylvania Avenue, in his presidential inaugural parade, in freezing temperatures and snow. As a matter of fact, I remember that we were all packed in the bus and it snowed from the time we left home until we reached our motel somewhere in Maryland. Hell, one of our buses even broke down somewhere on the highway along the way, but we finally got to our hotel. What an experience we had! Here we were in this motel, slot machines in the hallways and people all over the place. I guess the place was packed because of the storm and the inauguration. Talk about an education!

I remember that I had never seen some of the corps members before. I couldn't understand where the heck these guys came from. I didn't remember the bus stopping and picking them up. It seemed as though they came out of the woodwork to be in this inaugural parade. We sure filled up that street, Pennsylvania Avenue, and we made a good impression. After the parade, we were able to visit Washington, DC. We stayed in the DC area for the entire weekend. We even got an invitation to visit the White House. Once we got back home, these same corps members, who just appeared out of nowhere, seemed to disappear. To some of us, it will always be a mystery.

The corps was good for all of us. We made a lot of friends and traveled everywhere. We also got our first taste, other than Catholic school, of what real discipline was really like. The way the corps felt, if you didn't want to be in it, then get out. This was one place that no matter where you came from, whether you came from money or not, we were all treated the same and we seemed to take care of and watch over each other. Imagine teenagers standing at attention with your heels together and your toes at a forty-five degree angle, arms down to their sides, eyes front and no one talking or moving about until the drum major gives the command to move. I can remember those spring and summer nights out on the practice field, black flies and mosquitoes galore, and we were standing there waiting for that command. I can honestly tell you, I have never been with such a dedicated bunch of kids. I can remember that some of my school friends could not understand what kind of hold the corps had on us. To be treated like we were in the military! They couldn't believe it. Once, someone asked me, "What kind of a life is that?" Of course, this was not a corps member. They just could not understand the feeling of really being a part of something, everyone working toward the same goal, being the best that you could be, and everyone doing it together.

For me, like I said earlier, I started out trying to play the drums. What a joke! I was eight years old. I wasn't coordinated. I was lucky I could walk and chew gum at the same time. A few practices later, they asked if I would like to try and play a bugle. That same night, they put me in the horn section. I remember one corps member telling me that I will never be able to play that horn. Well, that did it for me. I started by just barely blowing that thing, but every day after school, I would practice and practice. I didn't have time to play outside or join any sports; all I did was play that horn. Within a couple of years, I became one of the best horn players in the corps. I can remember how Mom would come out and watch us march and listen to us play. She was so proud of us. I felt pretty good too playing the way I did. This was the one thing that I could do well, and no one disputed it or could take it away from me. God gave me a special gift, and it was playing that horn. My dad never once told me that I played well or that he was proud of me. He would help out with the administrative duties of the corps; he was on the board of directors, and he would volunteer to drive whenever the color guard needed drivers for color guard contests, but he never said that he was proud of any of us. Go figure! I never looked for any praise from him. I didn't play my horn for him or for his approval. I played it for me. It was my accomplishment and no one else's. It was my stress release from everything, and no one—no one— could take that talent that God gave me away, no one.

As the years went by, I kept going to school during the school year, and I also continued to wear that blue-and-gold drum corps uniform, and I watched as many of my friends, for whatever reason, would leave the corps. I stayed and kept marching and playing. I was one of the best buglers in the state, and it made me feel really good to play that horn. Then the shit hit the fan again. About every week, I would walk to my grandparents' house, my mom's mother and father, and on one of these Saturdays, I went over to wash their kitchen floor. I walked into the house, and my grandmother was walking around, obviously upset. I asked her what was wrong, and she said that *Pepere* was sleeping on the couch, and he wasn't waking up. Now mind you, my grandparents did not speak English. They only spoke French. I walked over to the couch and looked at my grandfather, and I just knew there was something not right with him. I shook him and noticed that he was kind of cold to the touch. I decided to call my dad. I told Dad that there was something wrong with Pepere, and I asked him if he could come over to their house. Dad showed up, looked at Pepere, and told me to go and get my mother.

On Saturdays, my mom would always walk to the hair salon downtown. I knew right where it was. I walked downtown and saw my mom with her head under a dryer. I told my mom that Dad sent me to get her and that there was something wrong with Pepere. Now at this time, my mom was pregnant. I walked with her to her parents' house, and Mom was huffing and puffing as we walked. We walked into their house, and my dad told her that her father had died in his sleep. You could have hit my mom with a two-by-four. She started crying, and I held her. She sat down in Pepere's rocking chair, which was in the kitchen. Then my mom's brothers and sisters started to arrive. Things really went downhill from there. My uncles and one aunt were rummaging through Pepere's cashbox. Hell, Pepere was still on the couch and these nuts were dragging shit out. What a bunch of vultures! Anyway, finally, the funeral director arrived to take my grandfather out of the house. They carried my grandfather out, put him into the hearse and then drove off to the funeral home. You think that things couldn't get any worse than they already were? Well, they did. That Murphy's law took over again. My mom and her brothers and sisters were all talking about what to do with *Memere*, and they all decided that Memere would come with us to our house. So my dad and I started to walk Memere out, and we got as far as the side steps off the porch. All of a sudden, Memere started to go down. My uncles ran over, picked her up, carried her, and put her on the same couch that my grandfather just died on. I guess that God had his own plan for Memere, because it was about three hours since I found my grandfather, and Memere died right there on that same couch. Now pandemonium set in. Things got really bad. My mom—remember, she was pregnant—was crying, and the funeral director came back to get my Memere. What a mess, but like I said, God took over, and we kept telling my mom that Pepere always took care of Memere, and he came back to get her, and now Memere was with Pepere in heaven. The funeral was unbelievable; we had both caskets together, Memere and Pepere in the same room at the same time. We had a double wake and funeral and buried both of them at the same time. In a way, it was absolutely beautiful. It was a real act of God's love. Now, no one had to worry about where or who Memere was going to be with. She was right where she belonged, right with her husband.

Like everything else in our life, this too passed, and life kept going for us. My mom had her baby, and now I had a baby brother. Everyone got back to their own lives.

During my high school years, I would get dismissed from school so I could play taps for the veterans' groups as they buried their comrades who died in someplace called Vietnam. That Vietnam thing will come later. For now, I was still in high school and still doing my thing, but I also had a part-time job working nights after school in the local shoe factory. Now that was different too. I got a lucky break and a couple of the supervisors in the shoe shop took a liking to me, so now I became a foreman on the night shift. I got paid seventy-five dollars a week to make sure that the night shift kept busy. Most of the workers were like me, high school students. It was all piecework for them. The more they worked, the more they made. If you needed the money, this is what you did. I had about fifteen people working that shift. Even back then, in my high school years, it seemed that I didn't have enough time for everything—the corps, working, school, girls, just not enough time for it all. I remember that on Friday nights we would work until about eight o'clock, and then we would have someone go out and get us lunch. That person would come back with a case of Colt 45 malt liquor. Now that's rotgut beer, but we didn't know any better. It was alcohol. We would eat, drink, and play cards until our shift was over at midnight. Then we would clean up and punch out for the night. We did this almost every Friday. Now mind you, I was not a big drinker. Sure, I snuck a few drinks at family weddings and all, and sometimes,

I would get to drink a beer or two, but nothing steady. I guess you would say that I would drink whenever I had the opportunity, and that wasn't much. By now, I did have a steady girlfriend, and she lived in the neighboring town. I used to walk to her house, because I was only fourteen or fifteen and I didn't have my license to drive. Hell, even if I did have a license, I didn't have a car anyway. After a while, her dad, who spoke mostly French, would ask if I wanted to play cribbage. I liked playing cribbage, so I would play cards with him. One night he asked me, in French, if I wanted to have a shot of scotch. I looked at him straight in the eyes and said, "Sure I would." So he gave me a glass of scotch with a touch of 7UP and a beer, usually Schlitz beer, as a chaser. Now let me tell you, did I ever like that scotch. It was the first time that I drank scotch, and it was love at first taste. It was great, and the beer chaser was a good mix. He would give me two or three of those, and I didn't care if I walked or not. Shit, I really didn't care if I was on foot or horseback. As a matter of fact, it really was the highlight of my night. I'd go to see my girl, but I really couldn't wait to play cribbage with her father. I would get feeling good. I'd be half in the bag, and I could care less about my girl, as long as he kept feeding me that scotch and beer. At the end of the night, I would kiss my girl good-bye, and I would walk back home, which was at least eight miles, feeling no pain at all. Once, my girl came right out and asked me if I was going over to her house to see her or her father. If the truth be known, it was to see her father and get feeling good with him, but to keep the peace—and I wasn't a fool—I told her it was to see her. Hell, I did like the way she felt, and I loved making out with her. And the booze made me horny as hell. I can't tell you how many nights I'd walk home with the "blue balls." I didn't care; I had a good buzz going, and half the time I was shit-faced. It was all good.

    The corps continued to travel to towns throughout New Hampshire and in different states like New York, Massachusetts, Vermont, Connecticut, Rhode Island, Maine, and even Montreal and Quebec, Canada, marching and playing. We were pretty good for a bunch of kids from a hick town. I remember one time in New York City, we were staying at the Knickerbocker Hotel, the home of the famous Peppermint Lounge. Our rooms were on the tenth floor. We were all excited and were running everywhere. The chaperones had all they could do to keep us in line. We were in and out of the girls' rooms, and I remember hanging out the windows, throwing water balloons at pedestrians as they walked the sidewalk in front of the hotel. Some of the guys were walking on the ledges to get into the girls' rooms. What a time! While in New York, the whole corps went to Radio City Music Hall for a show. Man, was that cool. Seeing the Rockettes perform on that stage was quite a sight. And the highlight of their performance was all of them in a perfect chorus line doing their famous high leg kick as they danced. It was absolutely breathtaking. But I was about thirteen or fourteen years old, and I was kind of hanging out with one of the girls in the corps. She was also a horn player, and she and I would play duets. She was fifteen or sixteen years old at the time, and she had a set of boobs to die for. All I remember is that she wore this tight top and she had a great cleavage going. I really didn't care what was playing at Radio City because I was sitting next to her and I couldn't keep my eyes off her boobs. I was holding her hand, looking at those boobs, and man, was I in heaven. Because of our age difference, we didn't go out very long, but that was OK. We were, and always remained, good friends. I also liked it that my older sister was in the corps color guard. She would bring some of her friends home. A couple of these girls were real good-lookers and built like brick shit houses. One time, I had a water fight with one of them. It was one of those days that my dad was at the fire station and my sister had a friend over. I got messing around with her friend and started to use the kitchen sink sprayer, and we were spraying each other. Now, let me tell you that I had the better end of that deal, because I sprayed her and soaked her white blouse, and all you could see was her blouse sticking to her boobs. Now that was good! Yes, the corps had its great perks! I even got to go out with a girl from another corps. This girl was from Portsmouth, and she was at least sixteen or seventeen, and man, did she turn me on. She loved to just sit on the bleachers and raise one leg, and you could see all the way up her legs, and let me tell you, she had great legs! I hung around with her every chance I could. I guess the only reason she latched onto me was because I was the soloist of our corps, and she liked that because she was one of the color guard captains of her corps. As I got older, I noticed that girls from other corps were attracted to me because I was a really good horn player. Hell, one year I was named Mr. New Hampshire Drum Corps. I received this trophy and got my picture in the state regional newspaper. That was pretty cool and was another perk of being in the drum corps. You know, all of us in the corps were like a big family. It was nothing to get to a field contest, rush off the buses, and all change up into our uniforms right out in the open, together. Yes, girls and guys changing up together, and no one thought anything of it, no one.

I finally turned sixteen, and I got my driver's license. Now this was a great feat in itself. Do you think that the old man would ever take me out and teach me how to drive? Hell, no way. He didn't have time for that. Heaven forbid if he would take the time to teach his son how to drive. Good thing that I had an older brother. He would take me out into the fairgrounds and made sure that I knew how to drive. Hell, he even borrowed our friend's Chevrolet station wagon, and that is what I drove. So on my sixteenth birthday, I took my driving test in that blue station wagon and passed both the written test and the driving exam. Parallel parking that big old boat was a breeze. I passed with flying colors! I got back home, and I showed my mom my license, and then I asked Mom if I could take the family car for a ride. Well, Dad was working at the fire department, and the car was in our carport. Let me tell you about Dad's car. This was his baby. He always wanted this car so badly but never could afford it. One day, he and my mom went out, and they drove into our driveway with his dream car, a shiny black Ford convertible with a white roof and red leather interior. This was a real sharp-looking car. So I asked Mom if I could just take the car for a ride. Mom thought about it for a minute, and then she said, "Go ahead, but be careful and do not pick anybody up." Man, was I happy! I ran upstairs, changed, grabbed the car keys, and took that car for a ride, all alone. I felt like a king as I drove around the neighborhood. Then I decided that I would drive across town to a friend's house. Well, again, Murphy's law, if it could happen, it did happen. Yes, just as my luck would have it. I drove across town, onto a side street, and toward my friend's house, and all of a sudden, this guy driving an old green sedan ran a stop sign and hit me right in the passenger door. Yes, he T-boned me so good that I was forced to the left and hit a tree right in the driver's door. If that wasn't bad enough, I bounced off the tree and that old sedan hit me again in the right rear quarter panel. All I could think of was *My dad is going to kill me. Holy shit, what the fuck am I going to do?* Christ, I even thought of just running away. My dad's dream car was a complete disaster. His car was fucked up really good. The police came and asked me if I was OK, and all I could say was that my dad was going to kill me. The car got towed, I walked over to my friend's house, telephoned my mom, and told her what happened. She asked me if I was all right, and then she said, "Your father's going to be really angry." No shit, Mom. I just totaled his baby! Mom told me that I should call Dad at the station. God, did I ever hate the thought of that. Before calling my dad, my friend's mother was home, and she was making daiquiris in a blender. I looked at her and told her that I had to call my dad at the station and tell him what happened. She poured me a daiquiri and told me to drink it. I drank that alcoholic drink, white rum, and was all calmed down. I finally got up the courage to call the old man and told him what happened. To my surprise, there was a lot of silence on his part. Then he asked me where the car was. I told him that it was towed to a place down the end of the road. He never yelled or anything, and all he said was that he would talk to me later. I knew that I still wasn't out of the shits yet, but at least he wasn't yelling at me, at least not yet. I did tell him that the cops came and they did cite the other guy because he ran a stop sign and hit me. I knew that he would talk to the police and that they would tell him exactly what happened. I can only tell you that this was the first and last time that I ever borrowed the family car. I was working now, and all I did was save my money, and eventually, I bought my own car.

I finally saved enough money and bought a '57 purple two-door Chevy coupe with a three-speed Hurst floor shift. Was I ever proud of that car! It was like the cat's ass to drive that hot rod around. I had it all decked out with loud dual exhaust, oversized tires, and a great stereo radio. I would drive over and pick up my girl, and we would drive to the beach. Yes, the car smoked a little, but who cared? It was my car, and I didn't give a shit about a little smoke, but my girl sure did. She would always get carsick, and I always had to pull off the road so that she could puke. What a great time. She sure was a great date. She would throw up all the time, no matter where we went. Again, my luck anyway, Murphy's law! I was getting used to this kind of shit happening to me. It became kind of a joke. I had to continue to work just to keep that car on the road. One time, I parked the car in my driveway, shut it off, and didn't put the parking brake on. While I was in the house I noticed, out of the corner of my eye, that my car was rolling down the driveway backwards, right across the street into my uncle's hedges, and right up to his front steps. There was always something—the shifter, the car smoked too much, wouldn't start—hell, if it could happen, it did. I finally had to get rid of it, but that was later.

On Sundays—like I said earlier, we were Catholics, and my parents were extremely religious—we were expected to go to church. Heck, all during our grade-school years, we would go to church as a family. Well, as we got older, my older brother and I would leave for church but never make it. We would make it as far as Main Street and end up at Larry's Donut Shop. We called it Larry's chapel, and we would meet our friends and hang out there until Mass was over. We made sure that one of us would walk up the street to the church and get a few weekly church bulletins. We would bring the bulletins home so that our parents would think that we went to church. So much for going to church.

Our corps became well known and respected. We now had played at the New York World's Fair and at the Montreal Expo, which was the Canadian World's Fair. Hell, we played at Madison Square Garden and Boston Garden and marched in every one of Boston's St. Patrick's Day parades. In spite of all our accomplishments, we kept losing members to the armed forces or through attrition. Once a member reached the age of twenty-one, you could no longer be an active marching member in the corps. At one point, it became hard keeping good members. We kept going, day after day, week after week, practicing, marching, and playing. Some might think that this could get pretty boring, but let me tell you, it didn't. The corps' repertoire changed as each year or season went by, and with the new seasons came new songs, and with each new song added to our repertoire came a new challenge for me. For some reason, I couldn't play our songs the same way twice. I had to either add some high notes or slur along. It was fun for me and rough for the bugle instructor. We all muddled through it, and it came out all right. And the marching and maneuvering changed with each season. At one point, we had the color guard doing a pretty good cancan. Yes, the corps was far from boring.

After practices, a bunch of us would get together for burgers and frappés. We would travel as a group and would be out all hours of the night. Our parents didn't seem to mind because we were together. It was kind of funny; we would rather be together, hanging out, than to be with our girlfriends. Of course, if your girlfriend was not in the corps, like mine wasn't, then they could not understand why we were the way we were—why we were not with them and why we would rather be in the corps, marching and playing. I really felt good playing that horn. And when I was playing, I was somebody. I was the soloist! Don't get me wrong, we had other soloists, but I was kind of the top dog. This was something that I did my best at, and everyone knew it. One time we had a field contest in Wells, Maine. We went out on the field and had a real good performance. We were marching off the field, and a girl, a high school senior from our school who was a very good-looking girl and really popular, walked over to me and gave me a kiss on my cheek and told me that I was great. I always had kind of a crush on her and never thought that she even knew who I was. Man, was I in heaven! Having her notice me and giving me a kiss in front of everybody made my day!

Well, things kept going, and eventually, after ten years, I had to make a decision. I was getting ready to graduate from high school. I had to make up my mind what I wanted to do: go to college or go in the service. Of course, I really didn't like school very much, especially since I spent eleven years at a Catholic school. Plus, my parents didn't have the money to put me through college, and back then school loans were hard to get, especially with my grades. I did not like to study, and I just got by. Shit, I told you that between the corps, work, and school, it was hard to find time to do my school homework. I had a cousin, a girl cousin whom I was really close to. We grew up together. She conveniently lived across the street from us, and she was in the same classes that I was in. One day I was in so much of a hurry to get my homework done, I took her paper and copied it. Remember that Murphy's law thing—yes, I copied her homework, and not realizing it because I was in such a hurry to get it done, I even copied her name. Now, let me tell you, did I learn a valuable lesson. I handed in my homework, and at the end of the school day, the teacher, a high school nun, addressed the classroom and said that she got everybody's homework but mine. She walked over to my desk, with all the homework papers, and asked me in front of the class where my homework was. I told her that I handed it in with all the other students. She looked at me and said that she had everyone's paper, but mine was not one of them. I told her that she must be mistaken or she misplaced it. She said no, she had everyone's and that it was a funny thing because she had two homework papers from my cousin, and that one of the papers appeared to have my handwriting. Well, what I did in my haste to get it done was not only copy her paper, I also copied her name! Now how stupid was that? Yes, David was in trouble again. This time for cheating on my homework. I couldn't win to save my soul. Luckily, I was older now and it was high school. The nun made me make up the homework, and that was that. So much for being too busy. I can tell you that, to this day, I never lived that down. I was the joke of the class.

At eighteen years old, I made up my mind. In May of that year, I drove to the local induction center, took my physical, and joined another corps, the United States Marine Corps. Let me tell you, were my parents thrilled. No, not really. With that thing about Vietnam going on, things at my house got pretty heavy. As a matter of fact, things were not good all around. My girlfriend could not figure out why I stayed in the drum corps after enlisting in the marines. She never could figure me out. She hated the idea that I joined the marines without talking to her first. Shit, she hated everything I did, especially being and staying in the drum corps. Well, I stayed in the corps for the rest of the summer, practicing, marching, and playing all over the place. We were really good that year. We had a great repertoire of songs. I played a lot of solos, and everyone jelled. Everybody loved to listen to us play. Then in the fall, September came, and I had to report for duty with the United States Marines. So I played in my last drum corps competition, said my good-byes, handed in my bugle and drum corps uniform, and left my friends, my girl, and my family. Giving that bugle up was like losing my best friend but it was time to go.

Now I belonged to another corps, a larger corps, and donned a new uniform, my third uniform. Talk about a scary situation. Unbeknownst to me, my whole life was about to change in a big way and forever.

Chapter 4

Marine Corps Boot Camp

1968

You know, I was so proud to be a marine and to serve my country. There are so many slogans about the marines—"Once a marine, always a marine," "First to fight," "A few good men," and so many more—but the best quote that was ever made about a marine came years later from the president of the United States, Ronald Reagan. In 1985, President Reagan said, "Some people spend an entire lifetime wondering if they made a difference in the world. But the marines don't have that problem."

At first, everything was great. Everything was lackadaisical. We left home and met a bunch of other recruits in Portsmouth. The marine recruiter was there. He was friendly and smiling. He probably was smiling because he knew exactly what was in store for us. Now that I think of it, he was smiling like the cat that caught and ate the bird. He shook our hands and wished us luck. Little did we know that where we were going, we were going to need all the luck that we could get.

Before leaving for the service, I signed a form to have two-thirds of whatever money I was making sent directly to my home. So the marines sent most of my monthly pay to my parents' house. I asked my parents if they would deposit the money for me into my bank account at the parish credit union, which I had since I was fourteen. Mom said that she would make sure the money would go into my account. I felt good about that.

Now, back to our bus trip south. We were driven to the Boston airport, got on this big airplane, and flew south. Now, that was the first time I ever flew on a plane. I loved it! The excitement of taking off and flying in the air. We landed somewhere in South Carolina and got on a bus. We were all talking, smoking, meeting new people, telling stories, and having a good old time. We were all heading for a place called Parris Island. I'll never forget it as long as I live.

Late at night, or maybe early in the morning (all I know is that it was still very dark outside), the bus pulled into the gates of the United States Marine Corps Recruit Depot, Parris Island, South Carolina. We were driving through those gates, which were guarded by two uniformed marine sentries. Some of the guys on the bus were still smoking, talking, and laughing. The bus came to a quick stop. The door flew open, and all I know was that this two-legged raving maniac dressed in a really starched-out marine uniform walked onto the bus and started yelling and screaming. Hell, you could have cut yourself on the heavy crease he had on his trousers. He was calling us all kinds of names and swearing. The next thing I know, this raging madman walked over to a guy who was sitting in front of me and slammed this guy's head through the bus's side window. That really got our attention! You could have heard a pin drop.

We were all assholes and elbows, running off the bus, standing at attention outside in the dark, and because of being in the drum corps—thank God—I had an advantage over most of these guys. I at least knew what attention was. Some of these poor bastards, who never knew anything about military courtesy or discipline, got a real eye-opener. Now we had three of these raving maniacs dressed in marine corps uniforms, who called themselves drill instructors (DI), all yelling at us at once. They called us everything under the sun. None of us dared move. After a while, they marched us into a large room, and we were told to stand at attention in front of these tables and not move. Then we met the senior drill instructor. He strutted around like a peacock, and let me tell you, was this guy mean. He wasn't a tall or big man, but he was all business. You just knew that he could walk the walk and talk the talk. When he opened his mouth, we listened and moved. One thing about the marines was that we were all treated the same. There was no prejudice at all. Whether you were white, black, Hispanic, Indian, Oriental—hell, it didn't matter; we were all the same—a bunch of fuckups.

They kept us up all night long, dictating, delegating, yelling, screaming out orders, and really belittling us. It seemed that they tried to get us to defy them. But let me tell you, they put the fear of God in all of us. We were told to take off all our clothes, except our Skivvies and socks. Then they took a black Magic Marker and wrote a big number on our chest. We had to empty the contents of our wallets and take off any, and all, jewelry. I had a high school class ring that I couldn't take off. It was too small for my finger. I tried to get it off, but it would not come off no matter what I did. Well, that didn't go over big, and the next thing I knew, they cut that ring off my finger. Then these drill instructors went to each and every one of us and inspected what we had. I kept my holy medal on, and the DI tore it off my neck and made me do push-ups. Then he took my girlfriend's picture from my wallet and held it up and told everyone to say good-bye to all our sweat hogs back home. He then tore the picture in half and threw it on the floor. Then they told us to line up and placed us in front of these bins and began issuing us military clothing—fatigue uniforms, caps, Skivvies, socks, and field boots. They told us to pack everything into the issued green seabag (duffel bag). We also had to pack our civilian clothes away and prepare to mail all our civies home. Then came our haircuts. They took it all down to the scalp. Now, where in hell did these guys ever get a license to cut hair? What degree did they have? How hard is it to learn to take an electric clipper and give everybody a buzz? Who knows? No exceptions, everyone lost all their hair. We all looked the same—a bunch of cue balls walking around in our Skivvies and socks. And you better not talk or utter a word because these DIs would be on you like stink on shit, because all we were to these DIs were maggots, ladies, pukes, scumbags, numb nuts—you name it, we were it!

Now came the medical exam. This was quite an experience. Still dressed in only Skivvies and socks, we were marched into this big room and lined up. We had these guys dressed in white—who the hell knows what they were—on both sides of us. I guess that they were navy corpsmen, male nurses. Who the hell knows? Like I said, first they wrote a large number, with a black marker, across our chest. You had better not try to rub it off either. Then we had these people on both sides of us, these corpsmen, giving us injections with these air-gun-type needles. You better not flinch because they'll rip open your arm as you walk past them. I don't know how many shots I got, but my arms sure were sore. Some of these poor bastards just fainted at the sight of these air type shot-guns.

As morning came about, they had us dress in our fatigues and lined us up at attention outside in front of the building, with all our gear in the seabag. Again, you better not move or talk. By now, we had been up all night, jumping through hoops for these DIs. Then we were issued our M14 rifle and a fire bucket. I said to myself, *What the hell is this bucket for and why do they call it a fire bucket anyway? Don't they have any of those big red trucks around to put out fires?* I guess not; we needed these damn buckets. After all this, they marched us to our new home. We were in the Third Battalion, Platoon 3029. Some called it Disneyland, but it was far from Disneyland. The barracks was a two—(2) story red brick building. It was a new section of Parris Island, hence the nickname Disneyland. From the moment we stepped foot in our barracks, we were run around, yelled at, sworn at, and again, called all kinds of names, including, "You are not even a fucking human being, you are all equally worthless pieces of amphibious shit." Then we were made to perform all kinds of exercises—push-ups, squat thrusts, knee bends, up and down—you name it, we were doing it. They referred to us as ladies, scumbags, fuckups, pukes, and pussies. Where the hell did they ever come up with all these names that came out of their mouths so naturally? You name it, they called us everything you can think of. Then they had us make our racks (beds). And let me tell you, if you didn't make that rack the way they wanted it, you would pay for it. They would tear your bed apart, make you do more push-ups, and then remake the bed. Then we had to unpack our seabags and pack everything into our wooden footlocker. Again, you better pack it the right way, or there would be hell to pay, and if one recruit made a mistake, the whole platoon would pay. They had issued each of us a padlock and you better lock your footlocker with it and it better be locked at all times or there would be hell to pay. I remember that one time I saw this DI walking the squad bay and he noticed that someone's footlocker had an open lock. This DI flipped out and went crazy and opened that boots footlocker and threw everything from inside his footlocker all over the squad bay. He was yelling and screaming and calling this boot "shit for brains, numb nuts" and everything else he could think of. We all paid for that boot's mistake. I have never done so many push-ups and squat thrusts in my life. And if the DI wasn't satisfied, then we did these wonderful little exercises, like jump over the rack, pick up the footlocker, place the footlocker over your head, under the rack, on the floor, off the floor, roll around, roll around on your back, on your stomach, on your back again—all kinds of little maneuvers. Anything that the DI could dream up we did it, until he finally told us all to get undressed and get into our racks. Then he would tell us not to move, and he would say, "Good night, ladies."

Morning would come, and did our DIs know how to wake up a bunch of new guys. At zero dark thirty, they would come in yelling and screaming, throwing garbage cans. You name it, they did it. This went on for nine glorious weeks, which actually seemed like a lifetime. Boot camp used to be thirteen weeks, but because of the Vietnam war and the quick turnaround of troops, for whatever reason, they changed it to nine weeks so that we could get to that place called Vietnam that much quicker.

Pull-ups, sit-ups, squat thrusts, close-order drill, right flank, left flank, to the rear, manual of arms, left shoulder, right shoulder, port arms, and you better know the difference between your right and left, or there would be hell to pay. At first, you could not figure out what in hell the DI was saying. What kind of language was this? Was he talking a foreign language or what? We would be marching, and all you heard was something that sounded so foreign—"hwan, hup, threep, fo, yo, lef!" You are thinking to yourself, *What kind of shit is this? What language is he talking anyway? What did I get myself into?* "yo, right o left, right o left, hey, do your lo!" How the hell do I know if I can lo? I tried to follow the guy in front of me, and I hoped to God that he "loed." It seemed that every DI had their own language for cadence. And you better not mess up. We had this one DI who liked to play a little sadistic game of hitting you in the throat. After he hit you, instinctively, you would put your hands up to your throat because you're choking. He would then punch you in the stomach, right in the solar plexus. Now you go down to your knees because you are doubled over and you can't breathe. This nut then picks you up by the throat, and it starts all over again. If you flinch, he gets pissed, and he hits you harder. When he first did this to me, instinctively, I went to grab my throat because I could not breathe, then the punch in the gut and my eyes watered up, but I didn't go down. I wanted to kill this sadistic bastard, and he just kept it up. He finally gave up because I wouldn't give him the satisfaction of going down to my knees. Not for this prick! He kept yelling, "You want to hit me, don't you, pussy?" I kept replying, "no, sir!" I really wanted to hit this fucking nut, but

I knew that if I did, the shit would hit the fan, and I'd be locked up in the brig.

At night, once lights go out inside the barracks, one of us would be on fire watch. We all took turns on fire watch. You would walk around in the dark wearing your combat boots, Skivvies, tee shirt and your combat helmet, carrying a flashlight and your fire bucket. Heaven forbid if something happens while you're on fire watch. If someone was where they weren't supposed to be or if someone escaped, your ass would be grass, and the DI was the lawn mower. When it was my turn and I walked about in the dark, I could hear some of these guys crying. Luckily for me, nothing out of the ordinary ever happened. During our boot camp, we had three marines who committed suicide in the latrine. Two hung themselves, and one boot cut his wrist and bled to death. Then we had a couple of boots who snuck out at night and went AWOL (absent without leave). I don't know what the hell these two guys were thinking. It's a military training base. Where the hell are you going? Doesn't one think that perhaps the military police might be out there? And that is what happened. They were picked up on base by the MPs, and after coming out of the brig, they went to Motivation Platoon and had to start boot camp all over again. Motivation Platoon was not a nice place to be. All day long, these guys would be running and carrying and hauling telephone poles around on their shoulders. No thank you! I didn't need that shit. Things were pretty tough as it was.

Each day we heard and did the same old shit. We heard the same things. They told us about this guy named Charlie, in Vietnam, who was going to kill us. Hell, I didn't even know anyone by the name of Charlie. Why the hell was this guy going to kill me? We drilled and marched. We ran all over the place singing these crazy cadences, and we had to repeat what the DI was singing, like "I don't know what I've been told, Eskimo pussy is mighty cold."

Now that was a no brainer! Who the hell came up with that?

> Ain't no use in lookin' down.
> Ain't no discharge on the ground.
> Ain't no use in lookin' back
> 'cause Jody's got your cadillac.
> Ain't no use in feelin' blue
> 'cause Jody's got your lady too.

Then we would count cadence as we marched. The DI would yell out, "Count cadence count," and we would all yell, "One." And he'd say, "A little bit louder."

"Two."

"Still can't hear you."

"Three."

"Starting to get better."

"Four."

"Now I can hear you."

"One, two, three, four, we love the Marine Corps." And we kept this up for weeks.

> If I die in the combat zone,
> box me up and send me home.
> Pin my medals upon my chest,
> tell my mother I've done my best.
> Lay my body six feet down
> until you hear it touch the ground.

And then one of my favorites was

> Everywhere we go
> people want to know
> who we are,
> where we come from.
> We came from an island.
> They call it an island
> Parris Island.

And, depending on which DI was drilling us, came another version:

> Everywhere we go, oh,
> people wanna know, oh,
> who we are
> and where we come from,
> so we tell them
> we are Marine Corps,
> mighty, mighty Marine Corps.

Lef-right-lay-F,
lef-right-lay-F,
gimme some, gimme some,
PT, PT gotta have it.
Oh yeah.
Lef-right-lay-F,
Lef-right-lay-F.

And another one we sang was

I'm on a trip to a hostile land,
To risk life and limb for Uncle Sam.
Don't know how long I'll be gone.
Don't know if I'll make it on home.
But I need to get out of this place,
'Cause I already stared death in the face.
But I moved around him with style 'n' grace,
Not leaving a step for him to trace.

And finally this is one of the best:

I love working for Uncle Sam.
Let's me know just who I am.
One, two, three, four, United States Marine Corps.
One, two, three, four, I love the Marine Corps.
My corps,
your corps,
Marine Corps
feels good.
Mmmm good.
I love the Marine Corps!
Ho Chi Minh is a son of a bitch,
Got the blue balls, crabs, and the seven-year itch.

For weeks, this was all we did. On about the third week, we were introduced to another goodie, the gas chamber. Now this was a lot of fun. The way that this little exercise was supposed to work was the DI was going to lead us into this gas chamber, which was filled with chlorobenzylidene malononitrile, known as CS gas, a nonlethal substance that is used in all branches of the military and by police for riot control. We were told that we would be wearing our gas mask as we entered the chamber, and when told by the DI, we would take our gas mask off. Now what the hell was this? Was this guy Charlie going to gas us, or what? Anyway, each boot was supposed to spend three to five minutes without our gas mask so that we could experience the effects of being gassed. Yeah right! We walked into this chamber, and the DI told us to take off our masks, and let me tell you, if you didn't take it off, they would rip that mask right off your face. This three—to five-minute thing, bullshit! They made us take off the masks and, after a while, put the masks back on, then take it off again. Now my eyes were watering, I could hardly breathe, I couldn't see, and I was getting sick to my stomach. Guys were puking and coughing and choking, and it didn't make any difference at all. Some of these boots were on the floor, in a bad way, but it didn't make any difference. We had to take our gas masks and put it on top of our heads. Now, some of the boots were really out of control and started running out of the chamber. Well, guess what? They ran out, and another DI quickly pushed them back in. It seemed like we were in this chamber for over one-half hour. The DIs kept yelling at us to keep the mask off and were calling us all kinds of names. We could barely breathe and were all coughing uncontrollably. Then the DI told us to put our arms down to our sides and walk out of the chamber. What a freaking ordeal. My skin was burning, my face was burning, I could not see at all, and my eyes were watering so much that you thought that I was in a shower. I walked out, and I tried to regain my composure and stand at attention. The DI who was outside made sure that you definitely had more than your taste and experience of the gas. They kept us standing there until everyone went through the chamber, and then they marched us off. That night, most of us were too sick to eat, but we still had to eat something, or else. Once back in the barracks, the gas smell was everywhere, because it was on all our fatigues. All you could smell was that gas. It made you sick! Who the hell could sleep?

Then they had us study and memorize our general orders. There were eleven general orders, and you better know each and every one of them.

1. Take charge of this post and all government property in view.
2. Walk my post in a military manner, keeping always on the alert and observing everything that takes place within sight or hearing.

3. Report all violations of orders I am instructed to enforce.
4. To repeat all calls [from posts] more distant from the guardhouse than my own.
5. Quit my post only when properly relieved.
6. To receive, obey, and pass on to the sentry who relieves me all orders from the commanding officer, officer of the day, officers, and noncommissioned officers of the guard only.
7. Talk to no one except in the line of duty.
8. Give the alarm in case of fire or disorder.
9. To call the corporal of the guard in any case not covered by instructions.
10. Salute all officers and all colors and standards not cased.
11. Be especially watchful at night and during the time for challenging, to challenge all persons on or near my post, and to allow no one to pass without proper authority.

The DI would walk up to you and just pick a general order out of his head, and you better be able to tell him what that general order was verbatim.

Then it was time to go swimming. They told us that marines need to know how to survive in the water. Now, what in the hell are we doing going in a pool with all our gear on? They said that we were going to tread water. We had to jump in the water fully dressed in flak jackets with all our gear, and once in the water, we had to start taking our gear off. Now, let me tell you, do you really think that everybody could swim and tread water? Some of these poor bastards jumped in and sank right to the bottom of the pool. We were supposed to take off our pants and put them up in the air over our head and fill them full of air, making a float out of them. Do you think it worked? What in hell were these DIs thinking of? All I could think of was, *Are they trying to drown us?* What kind of an exercise was this? We were supposed to be getting trained to go to Vietnam and fight. Did Charlie have a pool? Were there pools all over Vietnam? What the hell was the sense of this? Anyway, luckily, I knew how to swim. And I figured out that if I tied the ends of my pants in a knot, maybe I could get enough air in my pant legs to use them as a float, and that's exactly what I did. So much for swimming!

Then finally, the confusion seemed to stop, and you realized that everyone in our platoon became in sync; our hands, body, feet, and mind—all worked as one big machine, a team. But getting there was painful. I remember one time, I had a shit-eating grin on my face, and the DI went up one side of me and down the other. He had me doing all kinds of wonderful things, and finally, he took his little swagger, which was made of metal, and hit me across the ribs. Did that hurt! Son of a bitch, did I want to get this bastard. He must have broken two of my ribs, and man, I was in some kind of pain, but all you could do was bear it. I wasn't going to give him the satisfaction of knowing that he hurt me, that I was in pain. Fuck him! I would have given anything if I could hit him and get away with it, but I knew better.

Meals were a real treat too. You better like rabbit, because that's all the chicken you're going to get. Guys thought that this white meat we were eating was chicken, but actually, it was rabbit meat. You better eat everything you take, or you'll pay a price. Another little tidbit about the food, they laced it with saltpeter. Well, you couldn't get a hard on if you had to. All the food, including the C rats which would be issued later in Vietnam, was laced with saltpeter. And for God's sake, you better not talk while in the chow hall, or your ass will be grass and your DI will again be the lawn mower. And if you're a smoker, they'll give you a chance to go out and smoke, but you better make sure to take your fire bucket or else. And damn, do not throw your butts on the ground, or you'll be eating them. I remember one time that they let us go out for a smoke break. One of the boots was talking or mumbling about something. The DI came around and made all of us put our buckets over our head, and we had to continue to smoke, by the numbers, with the bucket over our heads. I don't know if you have ever done this before, smoke with a bucket over your head, but let me assure you that it sure does get you sick in a hurry. You have never seen so many guys with green faces, puking their guts out. Then we had to clean up our puke. Lot of fun! And they say that you'll have *free time*. Right! Every Sunday we were supposed to have some free time to go to a religious service, do our laundry, clean our rifles, and shine our boots. My ass, you'll have free time. You get yourself outside and wash your clothes in this big horse-trough-type of basin, shine your boots, and polish your brass, and your rifle better be immaculate. If the DI sees anything out of place at all, you're on the floor, doing push-ups and everything that goes with it. There better not be any Irish pennants on your fatigues either. An Irish pennant was lint or hanging threads. God forbid if you had any of

these, because if you did, you would be called a shit bird or Joe Shit
the Rag Man.

Then came the physical training and obstacle course, which today
is called the Crucible. We did rope-climbing; the slide of life, which
was a three-story rope hand-and-foot descent over a body of water; and
confidence course, which was a series of rope climbs combined with
a three-story log climb. They trained us in hand-to-hand combat and
fighting using the pugil stick, which is a five-foot long stick with large
hard rubber-wrapped ends. We would pair off and beat each other silly
with these things. And if you did not hit your opponent hard enough,
the DI would beat you. And he'd tell you how that guy, Charlie, was
going to get you. Who the hell is Charlie anyway?

The seventh week was at the rifle range. This was a great time.
The first week at the range was called snapping in. They had us sitting
on the ground and told us that they were going to snap us in. Well,
during this little exercise, they taught us how to properly hold our rifle
for firing in a sitting position. I watched as one DI walked over to a
boot (that's what they called us) and I guess this boot wasn't doing the
right thing; his pose was not right and his knee was too high and where
it should not have been, so he stepped on his knee to get his knee
down. All you could hear was *snap!* Yes, he snapped that boot in real
good. Of course he broke the boot's knee! No problem, the ambulance
arrived and carted the boot off to the infirmary. I knew this boot really
well as he and I joined the marines on the buddy system, which means
that we signed up together. After he got out of the hospital, he had
to start boot camp all over again. I really felt badly for him. I never
saw him again until much later in 'Nam. You know, anything that you
can imagine, they would do to us. The Marine Corps' attitude was to
tear us down any way they could and, supposedly, build us back up as
marines. There were some pretty sick individuals. We practiced and
shot and performed butt detail for two weeks. Oh, what's butt detail?
Well, it's down behind the targets, scoring the shots. Everyone gets to
play butt detail. Then at the end, record day, when you actually shoot
for your official record.

Then we go back and do more marching and maneuvering and
take a nice ten-mile hike to Eliott's Beach. This is a nice conditioning
hike, with all our gear. Great fun! You better make this, or else. They
forced-marched us through a swamp, and you better not fall in the
water, and if you did, they would make you do it all over again. Then

we have physical training with our rifles. Hold your rifle over your head, over to your side, in front of you, and you better not waiver or let your rifle down before the DI told you to. And you better not ever call your rifle a gun, or there would be hell to pay. They had this saying, and they made us all say it together, "This is my rifle, and this is my gun." Just think what that means. Your rifle was your rifle, and when you say *gun*, they had us grab our dick and balls. "This is for fighting, and this is for fun." Again, they made us grab our balls when saying *fun*. These DIs had all kinds of wonderful little sayings and songs. You wondered, *Where the fuck did they ever come up with this shit?* At the same time, they made us memorize the Rifleman's Creed. This again, just like your general orders, was beat into your head. Every boot marine must know the creed. The first part of the Rifleman's Creed goes like this: "This is my rifle. There are many like it, but this one is mine. [You better have a name for your rifle too.] It is my life. I must master it as I must master my life. Without me, my rifle is useless. Without my rifle, I am useless."

I think that you get the idea. It's all about kill or be killed. There is more to the creed, but the beginning is the most important part, and you better know it all.

Then there's bayonet training, and you better be aggressive, or else. They had these dummies hung up, and we had to run and attack them with the bayonet. Now if you didn't penetrate that dummy enough, they made you keep doing it until they were satisfied that you meant business. They wanted you to hit that dummy with your bayonet and rip that thing apart. Then more hand-to-hand combat training and more pugil-stick fights. Then on the eighth week, we were ready to take our physical readiness test. You better be ready, or you're going to start this mess all over at week one. Bullshit! I'm ready! Anything to get the hell out of here! The whole thing—confidence course, slide of life, and a nifty newcomer, crawling face up, on your back, holding your rifle on your chest as you crawl under barbed wire while some nut is firing an M60 machine gun, live fire, over your body. This was great fun. You sure as hell wanted to keep your butt down as far as you could into the ground.

After all this, the DIs seemed to start slacking off a bit. I think it's because we now were acting as they wanted us to, as marines. We had been through a lot and were getting closer to the end of this part of our marine training of boot camp.

On the ninth week, we had a final inspection, a drill competition, and then graduation day! By this time, we even had our own platoon song. "Move over because Platoon 3029 is coming through."

Graduation day, we earned the title *marine,* not ladies anymore, and once a marine, always a marine. Wherever we went, from this day on, we would always be a marine.

I never thought I'd see the day when I'd get away from these guys. Then like any other experience, eventually we graduated and were sent on to our next duty station for more training.

PLATOON 3029

THIRD RECRUIT BATTALION   M. C. R. D., PARRIS ISLAND, S. C.
SSGT. W. H. CLARK   SSGT. J. R. PHILLIPS   SGT. R. F. PORNOVETS
                         GRADUATED 26 NOVEMBER 1968

CHAPTER 5

AIT Training

Needless to say, most of us continued with infantry training, which they called AIT, which meant advanced infantry training. They were training us for that place called Vietnam. We were learning how to kill and how to stay alive.

We all packed up our gear and were shipped out. We arrived at a place called Camp Geiger, which is a satellite facility located within Camp Lejeune, in North Carolina, for AIT. This AIT training is the second stage of initial military training for boot marines after graduating from boot camp. It was an eight week training course that develops new marines into infantrymen "who can fight, survive, and win in combat situations." Our jungle training and amphibious training started. As far as the Marine Corps is concerned, no matter what your MOS (Military Occupational Specialty) is "Every Marine is, first and foremost, a Rifleman." We received instruction in combat marksmanship, proper use and handling of grenades, convoy operations, tactical formations, proper use of a compass and land navigation, and patrolling in hostile environments. This part of our training was a combination of outside classroom instructions, hands-on practical applications like throwing hand grenades, and live-fire exercises. We had to tear down our issued M-16s and 45 cal. hand guns and re-assemble them blindfolded. They even timed us and you better get it done quickly and correctly or the instructor would be on your ass yelling at you and telling you how much of a fuck-up you are and that you were going to get everyone around you killed by that Charlie fellow in Nam. Then they had these makeshift villages that supposedly resembled the villages in Vietnam. We were taught how to avoid booby traps, punji sticks, land mines and attack and raid the mock villages. Well, again, we had some nut as a platoon sergeant. This guy had just recently returned from Vietnam, where he served several tours. During his last tour of duty, he got severely wounded. At the entrance to our barracks, on a bulletin board, he posted photographs of his surgery. I don't know how many pictures there were, but they were gross. They were of his whole operation with his stomach cut wide open. Anyway, all we kept hearing was how we were going to die in 'Nam. How this guy named Charlie was going to kill us. That we only had a life expectancy of eleven seconds in Nam. It seemed that everyone but us knew Charlie. All I kept thinking to myself was, *Not this guy, not me. Charlie's not going to get me. I'm going to get back home in one piece, no matter what.* I was going over to this Vietnam place with all my body parts, and I vowed that I was going to come back home with all my body parts intact.

Anyway, we trained day and night. We kept doing skirmishes, village raids, night raids, and maneuvers, throwing hand grenades, using the M72 LAW (Light anti-armor weapon), watching out for all kinds of booby traps and mines. Let me explain one thing, which I think is very important, about the M72 LAW. It's a disposable weapon. You only have one shot with this thing and after that one shot, you throw it away. Makes a lot of sense to me. Why in hell would the marines give us a weapon that we can only use once and then throw it away? No clue, but I am sure that they have their reasons. We learned about the Viet Cong and how they acted and fought and about how sneaky and good they were in guerilla warfare. After four weeks, they finally let us go on furlough into Jacksonville, North Carolina. What a place! Here we were, most of us eighteen years old, going into this town that by now had its fill of boot marines. We went to this redneck bar, dirt floor and all. They no more wanted us in there than the man in the moon. All we wanted to do was to talk to a girl, maybe have a drink, dance, whatever. As soon as I opened my mouth, I was called a *yank*. It went downhill from there. These rednecks were still fighting the Civil War. I knew that if we got into a fight, we'd probably be locked up forever. Anyway, we decided to go back to base and go to the Enlisted Men's Club. Club, right! One pool table and a TV. Oh well, at least we didn't get into trouble and we were able to get served 3-percent-alcohol beer. You see, that's what the service served us, 3 percent beer. Hell, you couldn't get drunk if you had to. Shit, you could drown before getting drunk on that rotgut beer.

At the end of this stage of our training, which, like I said, lasted for eight weeks, they let us go home on leave before shipping us out to

Camp Pendleton and, eventually, to Vietnam. Well, that was quite a trip. I took a train, dressed in my Marine Corps uniform, from Jacksonville, North Carolina, to Washington, DC, had a layover in DC, then went from DC to Philadelphia, Philly to New York, and New York to Boston. What a ride! You've got to love the way people looked at us. We were lean, mean fighting machines, and most people did not like this Vietnam War. They didn't want us over there. They would stare at us in uniform like we were the enemy. It was great! Anyway, it was supposed to take about eleven hours to get to South Station in Boston, but it actually took over sixteen hours. Well, I told my parents that I'd be in South Station at such and such a time. Needless to say, I was late, and to my understanding, Dad was waiting, along with my mom and my girl, at South Station. Now, I have not been home since September, and when I got off the train in Boston, my dad was very upset. Yes, it was my fault that the frigging train was late. Sure, I was driving that train. Can't win for losing. It was a real nice car ride home. You know, once I was home, I couldn't wait to leave and get back to the Marine Corps. At least the corps kept me busy. I got so bored at home on leave. No one really had anything in common with me anymore. For over the last four months, all I did was train to kill people. I was full of piss and vinegar and anxious to get back so that I could do my job. There was this feeling of anxiety and nervousness about going over to Vietnam. You know that it's coming; you just want to get it over with. While I was home on leave, I would visit my girlfriend and her family. Her father and I would play cribbage, and he, again, served me that scotch drink with a beer chaser. Now that was the best part of being back home on leave, drinking and playing crib with him. While I was home, I took some money out of the credit union, and I bought a 1967 Ford Mustang convertible. It was a beautiful car, baby blue with a black top, and it had an automatic floor shifter. The front bucket seats were so comfortable, and it had a great stereo. I knew better than to leave that car at home, so I left it with my girl and told her to use the car while I was gone.

My leave lasted ten days, and I'll always remember my mom and dad, along with my girlfriend, taking me back to South Station so that I could get on the train for Camp Lejeune. Now remember, this could be the last time my parents ever saw me alive. I was leaving them to eventually go to Vietnam. My mom and my girl were very emotional, crying and saying how much they loved me and how proud they were of me, to take care of myself and be careful, and make sure that I came back home safely. My dad said nothing. Not even a hug, handshake, nothing. It was like he was put out because he had to drive me to Boston. Got to love it. Good old Dad never changed!

I got on the train and eventually got back to Jacksonville. While on this train ride, I met up with a couple of my brother marines. Then we took a cab back to base. We didn't stay there long. After a few days, they flew us out to California, to Camp Pendleton. What a big place. This was a marine base on the west coast, in Oceanside, California, which is between Los Angeles and San Diego. This was the time that we started to fine-tune our fighting skills. We were assigned to a staging battalion, where we would break up into platoons. We had fifteen days of intensive training before sending us to Vietnam. However, before our training started, they let us have a one-week furlough. A few of us decided to take a trip to Anaheim and go to Disneyland. We packed a ditty bag and left the base. Now that was quite a treat—four boot marines in uniform going to Disney. We got a motel room and visited the Magic Kingdom. Imagine going around Disneyland with another marine. Everywhere I looked, guys were with their families or their girlfriends, and we had each other. Oh well, we made the best of it and had a good time. We knew that once we got back to base, it would be all over. We then went to Long Beach and, eventually, to San Diego. I'll tell you now that this part of California was great. Long Beach was just what it says, it was a long beach. As far as one could see, white sandy beaches with no one on them. I could not believe that no one was at these beaches. It was beautiful to see. San Diego was a great city to visit. I know that someday, I will travel back to this area to visit.

After arriving back at base, the fun times were over. We started our intensive training. There was an old Korean war village that had been transformed into a Vietnam village, complete with deadly booby traps and mines. They were continually training us to fight and to survive and to get us ready to go into battle. We trained day and night, rain or shine, and conditioned ourselves to act as a fighting machine. We heard all about Charlie and the Viet Cong and how bad they were. We heard that we should never trust any of these people, even the kids. They loved killing marines and ambushing us every chance they could. We learned about their culture and their way of life and about the Vietnam girls, and to stay away from them and not to ever have sex with these girls because they all had venereal diseases. If you did have sex with them, you took the chance of catching something and having your dick fall off. What a great thought for an eighteen-year-old. We learned about the Vietnamese villages and rice paddies and about all their man-made mines and booby traps. You name it, they told us about it. They crammed information into our heads, day and night. I could tear down and put back together an M16 and a forty-five-caliber handgun with my eyes closed.

Well, the day came that we were going to be shipped out. This was it. This is what we trained for. We're leaving for Indochina and, eventually, Vietnam, but before leaving, we had to make out some type of will. Now, at eighteen years old, what the hell do you think? A fucking will? Are they trying to tell us something? The only thing I did, because I didn't own anything but a car and a few bucks in the credit union, was I left everything to my girl. I also had the paymaster now send most of my monthly pay, including my combat pay, back home to be deposited. Hell, where was I going to spend that money anyway? Ho Chi Minh didn't have anything that I wanted to pay for. Then they handed each of us something that I couldn't believe, a Geneva Conventions identification card. What the hell was this? I thought to myself. No way in hell was I going to become a prisoner of war. Why were they issuing this card to me? As I stated so many times, "This guy Charlie is not going to capture me. No way in hell." I am going to do my job and serve my country to the best of my ability, but I am not going to be anybody's prisoner, especially this Charlie guy.

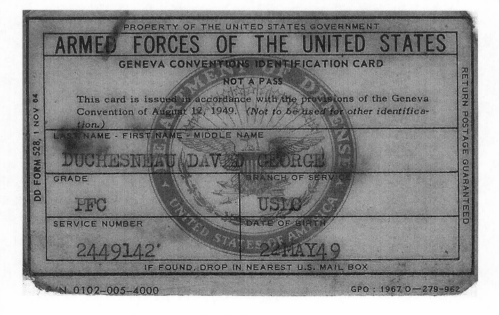

They had us up early, and everything we owned was packed in our green seabags. We lined up, like usual, and boarded a large commercial jet, Tiger Airlines. Can you imagine three hundred marines boarding this aircraft? I'll never forget the stewardess as we boarded. For some of these guys, this was to be the last American girl that they would ever see. We left California and landed in Hawaii. They let us get off the plane, but we had to stay in the airport terminal. Not being twenty-one, we couldn't drink. How about that, I can go and fight and possibly die for my country, but I couldn't legally drink. What a crock of shit. Someone said that going to war was a once-in-a-lifetime experience. Hell, I only knew that it was like I was writing Uncle Sam a blank check, which included my life for my country.

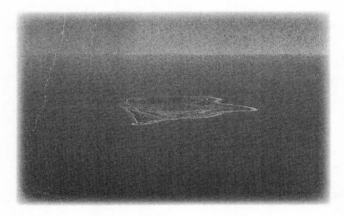

Three hours later, we left Hawaii and had to refuel the plane at Wake Island. Let me tell you, this is the smallest island located in the South Pacific that you can imagine. The only thing on Wake is the runway—that's it; nothing else, just the runway. We left Wake and landed in Atsugi, Japan. That was something, looking out onto the city of Tokyo as we landed. We didn't stay long, but I did get to see Tokyo by air.

I don't know how long it took us, but it seemed like days that we were on this plane. During the flight, we were all allowed three beers. Now remember, this is military alcohol, only 3 percent alcohol. Well, at least they let us have that. Now, it's the Marine Corps policy that marines are entitled to be rationed three beers a day. Remember that little tidbit for later. We landed at Kadena Air Force Base in Okinawa. We stayed here for about three days, getting ready to finally be shipped out to Vietnam. Now, what a place Okinawa was! Anyone who has been there knows about BC

Street. It's where all the local clubs and all the strip joints and prostitutes are. Hell, if you can't get laid in Okinawa, then there is really something wrong with you. Broads are all over the streets, selling their bodies. Anything goes here, and I mean anything. The smell of the city was really shitty. It was hot and humid, and these were all gooks, slant eyes. The only round eyes were the nurses on base. You couldn't get next to them unless you had a major medical problem. After three days of Marine Corps bullshit, the hurry-up-and-wait garbage, they finally ordered us to get ready for the flight to Da Nang airport. We were taken from Okinawa in another commercial 747 jet of Tiger Airlines. The flight lasted about three hours, and let me tell you, there wasn't much talking now. Now things were getting serious because we all knew that soon we will be in a hellhole for thirteen fucking months.

7B/MRL/drm
1650
9 Mar 1970

FIRST ENDORSEMENT on CG, III MAF ltr 1F/rad over 1650 of
2 Mar 1970

From: Commanding General, 1st Marine Division (Rein), FMF
To: Corporal David G. DUCHESNEAU 244 19 42 USMC
Via: Commanding Officer, Headquarters Battalion

Subj: Certificate of Commendation

1. I am proud to present this Certificate of Commendation
earned in combat operations in Vietnam. You may be sure
of my respect and appreciation.

E. B. WHEELER

CHAPTER 6

Vietnam

CHAPTER PREFACE

I would like to explain a few things before I go any further. My tour of duty in Vietnam was from March 1969 to August 1970. I have never talked about my Vietnam experiences, except about explaining what the country was like, the weather, the elements, the insects, the animals, and some of the natives that I came into contact with, the areas that I was exposed to, like Da Nang, Con Thien, DMZ, Cam Lo, Quang Tri, Dong Ha, Dong Ha Valley, China Beach, a few fire bases, Route 9 and Route 1, the Ho Chi Minh Trail, and the like. I have never talked about any battles, firefights, or any operations that I was involved in. There were several: Operation Maine Crag, Operation Virginia Ridge, Operation Pink Panther, Operation Idaho Canyon, and Operation Pipestone Canyon. I am going to attempt to describe, the best that I can, my recollection of the Vietnam War as I experienced it as a marine infantryman, a grunt. The dates and locations may be out of sequence, but the events are factual and actually occurred. All the names have been changed to safeguard everyone's identity, except mine. The units that I was assigned to are factual. There are many myths and misconceptions about the Vietnam War, but the most notable myth is that most Vietnam veterans saw combat. To the contrary, most soldiers in Vietnam did not see or were ever involved in combat. It is likely less than 30 percent of all who served in Vietnam were ever involved in combat. At the height of the war in 1969, there were approximately ten troops supporting every soldier carrying a rifle in the field. The rear echelon was very top heavy, much more than any other military force that was sent to war.

DEFINITION of a VETERAN

You would think that would be an easy question to answer. However, there is no standard legal definition of "military veteran." Most dictionaries define "veteran" as a person who has served in the armed forces. Using that definition, a person would be considered a "military veteran" with just one day of military service. Therefore, the best definition that I ever read of a veteran was actually written by an unknown author: "A Veteran is someone who, at one point in his life, wrote a blank check made payable to "The United States of America," for an amount of "up to and including my life." With this definition in mind, I, along with millions of other men and women who signed up in whatever Branch of Service to serve our Country, can honestly relate to this definition.

The average age of a marine who served in Vietnam was 19 years old. He was a short haired, tight muscled kid who was not old enough to buy beer, but was old enough to die for his country.

He was a recent high school graduate and was most likely an average student. He had a steady girlfriend who either broke up with him when he left for Vietnam or promised to wait for him to return home from halfway around the world.

Letter writing was a chore for him because his handwriting was poor and he had trouble spelling, but he could field strip his M-16 in ten seconds and reassemble it in the dark. He humped through the jungle and dug foxholes and could apply first aid like a professional. He would march until he was told to stop or stop until he was told to march.

He obeyed orders instantly and without hesitation. He was self-sufficient. He tried to keep his canteens full and his feet dry. He often forgot to brush his teeth, but never forgot to clean his M-16. He cooked his own meals, mended his own clothes and healed his own wounds.

He learned to use his hands like weapons, and his weapons like they were his hands. He could save your life-or take it—because that was his job. He did twice the work of any civilian, but only received half the pay, and he still kept his sense of humor in it all. He has seen more suffering and death than he should have in his short lifetime.

He cried in public and in private for friends fallen in combat and was not ashamed. He paid the price for our freedom. He is not a boy. He is a Marine, a fighting machine, who has helped to keep this country, and others, free.

He asked for nothing in return, except for friendship and understanding. He earned everyone's respect and admiration with his blood, sweat and tears.

March 1969

We finally landed in Da Nang. I'll never forget that smell when we walked off that plane. It smelled like someone had died, a rotten-food smell. The air was so humid and heavy. Now mind you, we were on the ground, in a war zone, and none of us had any weapons. Not one. What do you think was going on in our minds? What if the shit hits the fan? What do we do, throw our seabags at the enemy, or do we try and crawl inside the bag? Obviously, nobody gave a shit. We're just a bunch of boots coming in this country. Who cares? But I can tell you that I was scared shitless. I mean I was nervous, like a cat on a tin-roof. But that smell was everywhere. The heat was almost unbearable, and there we were in long-sleeve camo shirts. The first thing they did was march us all into this large hangar and show us a movie all about syphilis, the black syphilis. We were shown photographs of servicemen in some unknown hospital in Japan, with these large holes in their dicks. What do you think? They said that syphilis is prevalent with Vietnamese women and that we better stay away from babysan and mamasan. The odds of getting the clap was really good if you fool around with these women. Well, that was an eye-opener. Here we are in Vietnam, and we're here for a thirteen-month tour of duty, and the first thing they show is this. Where are our weapons? I think that right now the odds of us dying by this guy Charlie or the Viet Cong outweigh the clap. We have no weapons. What the fuck? The food we ate was laced with saltpeter. We couldn't get it up if we had to. Our marine escorts were real prizes. They had a stare on their faces that could freeze water. No expressions at all. They were as cold as ice. We also saw a lot of coffins stored in the back of one warehouse. I didn't know if these coffins were already filled or what. I thought to myself, *What a great fucking stinking place to be.* At my age, these are supposed to be the best years of my life. What a fucking waste being in this stinking hellhole.

Then we were led to a dormitory-type barracks, a one-floor wooden building with screens for windows. Still no weapons, and they told us that if the sirens go off, run to a shelter. What shelter? Where the hell is this shelter? Anyway, night came, and we could hear gunfire and loud explosions going off in the distance all around the area. You could see huge fire glows in the dark. I lay there on my bunk, wondering what would happen if that siren went off. Eventually, I fell asleep. Nothing appeared to happen during the night. No sirens. Thank

God for that! As morning came, they called out our names, and we were broken down into different companies. We were the replacements, replacements for the marines who died, who were going home, who were going on R&R—for whatever reason, we were the replacements.

I was taken over to the Third Marine Division supply sergeant and was issued a pair of jungle fatigues; jungle boots; a backpack; a helmet; a flak jacket; a mess kit; a gun belt; an e-tool (entrenching tool), which was a small folded shovel; two canteens; a rain poncho; a poncho liner, which is a camouflage lightweight blanket; extra socks; a bayonet; ammunition; hand grenades; and my M16 rifle. It's about time! I had been in this country for two days now, and finally, I got my rifle, hand grenades, and ammunition. Now I was ready for that Charlie fellow I've heard so much about.

They loaded us up in these troop carriers, sixby trucks, and they drove us north to Quang Tri. The reason that the Third Marine Division was in Quang Tri was because we were supposed to block the North Vietnamese Army (NVA) from infiltrating from North Vietnam to South Vietnam. The smell still didn't change, and the heat got hotter as each day went on. It had to be over one hundred degrees, and we just sat there sweating. Once in Quang Tri, we were again broken down into small groups. I was told to get on this troop-carrier helicopter, a large dual prop CH-46 Sea Knight, and was taken north, to Vandergrift Fire Base. I didn't realize that now I was right near the DMZ, the Demilitarized Zone, the dividing line between South and North Vietnam. I remember getting out of that chopper, and that carrying all my gear was a chore, making sure that you kept all your issued gear with you as you walked off the chopper. Do you think that this chopper

would stop running? Of course not. The chopper blades blew sand everywhere. Well, I made it off, with all my gear, and was met by my platoon sergeant. I learned that I was going to be assigned to Second Squad of B Company (Bravo), First Battalion, Third Marines, Third Marine Division. In other words, I was attached to Second Platoon, Second Squad of Bravo 1/3. Now that was a mouthful! It was the beginning of March 1969, and now I was in I Corps of South Vietnam, in Quang Tri Province. My squad leader, Mack, who was a Corporal, assigned me to the First Fire Team as a rifleman. Now, before arriving in 'Nam, I already knew that my MOS (military occupational specialty code) was 0311, which was a rifleman, or, as we were called, grunts or ground pounders. Most all marines were grunts. Anyway, I was introduced to the rest of my fire team and the squad, and I learned that I was a replacement for one of the marines who had just finished his thirteen-month tour and was sent back home. They all called home the World. Mack told me that our Commanding Officer, Captain Dan, was a real good man and that he, Captain Dan, was well respected by his men. That he was very proud of his men and he looked after each and every one of them. Knowing that we had a good CO made me feel more at ease because I heard stories about these CO's who were so gung-ho that all they cared about was making a good name for themselves and they could care less about their men.

Now, let me tell you, these guys that I just met looked scary. They were dirty and needed a shave and a bath. Their uniforms (jungle fatigues) were all faded, dusty, and dirty. These guys had a scary stare on their faces. Most of these guys really smelled bad. They definitely had their own body odor going. In plain English, they stunk! We had rednecks, blacks, southerners, midwesterners, Hispanics, Asians. Hell, we had more mix than an old hound dog. They had names like Tex, Chief, Bo, Badman, Mad Dog, Smoky, Whitey, Pooch, Dog, Chesty, Bro, Emmett, Brother Books, Lenny, Chu, Stone, Greek, and I was nicknamed Frenchy and, sometimes, Duke. I learned that most of these guys were drafted into the Marine Corps, and they couldn't believe that I enlisted. I quickly learned that these hard-core marines had their own slang language that I quickly had to learn just to survive. The enemy was called gooks, dinks, slants, slopes, zipper-heads and the little people. The Vietnamese people were also gooks or slant eyes; the girls were babysan, and the women were mamasan, and then we had the Montagnard. The head of these Montagnard villages were chiefs, and they were called papasan. Let me tell you, we had some of these South Vietnamese men who, supposedly, were our allies. They were assigned to our platoon, and they called them Kit-Carson-Scouts. I am here to tell you that these Vietnamese people appeared to be some of the nicest and friendliest people you could ever meet, and at the same time, you instinctively knew that they were also the most dangerous and deadliest people you could ever meet. We had to remember they were all Vietnamese and we were the foreigners who were patrolling in their country on search-and-destroy missions to kill the enemy, the North Vietnamese. Hell, you never knew who was a friendly gook or if they were sympathetic to the North Vietnamese or not. They all looked the same to me. They all looked like the enemy. As far as I was concerned, you couldn't trust these bastards if you had to, and you know what, we were supposed to be able to trust them with our lives. Well, not me, not this marine!

Well, I was quickly labeled an FNG, which was a fucking new guy, and they were going to show me how to stay alive in the bush. They taught me some of the language like, *boo-coo* (beaucoup), which meant a lot in French, and some of the Vietnamese words like, *Chieu Hoi*, which meant "surrender" or "give up," *Con Biet* (do you understand), *Di-Di* (leave, go, get out), *Di-Di-Mau* (get the fuck out), *Dinky-Dau* (crazy), *Du-Dit* (fuck you), *Lai Day* (come here), *Ti Ti* (small), number 1 (good), number 10 (bad), and a whole bunch of other bush lingo, like the South Vietnamese Army was ARVN, *Caca Dau*, which was Vietnamese for "I'll kill you," *Dung Lai*, which meant "stop" or "halt," and CYA, which was "Cover your ass in the bush." Now, remember that most Vietnamese spoke French as it was their secondary language because, originally, Vietnam was a French possession. So I had a little advantage that I could speak and understand enough French to get by in this godforsaken country.

You know that I never had any problems with anyone while in the corps. I got along with everyone. The whites and the blacks were all intermingled, and we got along really well. We actually had to because we had to count on each other to stay alive. We had several blacks in our squad, and our M60 machine-gunners fire team was made up of three blacks and one white guy. The only time that the blacks would get distant from their white fellow marines was when we would all get back to headquarters in Quang Tri or while we were on in-country R&R (rest and recreation). Then once we would stand down and rest for a couple of days, the blacks would all hang together and would have nothing at all to do with any of us whites. They would treat us like we were poison, like shit, and some whites would get all upset, and these racial slurs would start. Then the bullshit would start, and once we got back into the bush, all the bullshit stopped just as quickly as it started. After a couple of days, I realized that not only did you have to worry about your enemy, but the insects and bugs in this place were just as deadly. We had ants the size of small dogs and we had mosquitoes the size of small birds, and they carried all kinds of diseases, including malaria. We had snakes of all kinds, to include cobras, pythons, water snakes, and this small green snake, a bamboo viper, which was called the three-step snake, because if this snake bites you, you would die within taking three steps. We had big-ass spiders and scorpions. You name it, we had it. And the red ants, man, could they do a number on you. Remember, this whole area of the country was constantly being bombed, and all it did was bring these insects out of the ground. You never took your boots off at night because you never knew if something would crawl up inside your boots. Then I was told about Charlie, the gooks, the slant-eyed bastards. While patrolling and going through rice paddies and mountain villages, you had no idea if those pajama-wearing Vietnamese were either from the north or the south and if they were allies or sympathetic toward the North Vietnamese. Even the kids and the women (babysan and mamasan), you just didn't know. All I knew was that I was going to get through this and get my ass back home to the World. I wasn't going to let anything or anyone get me.

In the lowlands, you had elephant grass and these big-ass tigers to worry about, and in the mountain region, you had these big-ass rock apes. Vietnam had it all! We even had these big ass lizards and it was kind of funny because at night you would hear these lizards and these bastards sounded like they were saying "shit-bird" or "fuck you." So we called these lizards the "shit bird and fuck you lizards." Another thing about lizards and snakes is that people say if you cook and eat a lizard or snake that they actually taste like chicken. Well I am here to tell you that they are full of shit. Well, I don't know what kind of lizards or snakes that they ate. While in Nam, I ate both and they sure as hell do not taste like chicken. Any kind of shit that you could ever imagine was here. If it wasn't one thing like the heat, malaria, diarrhea, jungle rot, it was something else. After a few days, we were issued seven days of C rations, which meant that we had seven days of food. Now, let me tell you about this stupid food. First, it was all canned and packed and date-stamped 1949. Now think of this, this so-called food has been sitting inside these cans for twenty years. Each of the seven cartons (one carton per day) had some sort of a condensed breakfast meal, like eggs, ham, and lima beans, beans that soon became known as ham and motherfuckers, which most of us in the field hated to eat. Then we had a snack of a small can of peanut butter and these round crackers. That was a real treat. This peanut butter had more grease than the motor pool, and the crackers could be used as weapons. Man, were they hard. Then we had lunch that consisted of some sort of condensed chicken. Talk about heartburn city. Man, was that hard to get down. Then there was a can of spaghetti and who the hell knows what was in that. I guess it was supposed to be meatballs, but who the hell knows what it was. The only really good thing was a can of peaches and a can of pound cake. We even had a can of bread, if you dared to eat it. Once you opened the can, the bread would start to ooze out. It actually was scary. I always wondered, if one of these cans ever exploded, would the bread fly out all over the place? Then, each box had a piece of chocolate, a pack of hot chocolate, pack of dried coffee, sugar, and powdered milk for your coffee, toilet paper, chewing gum—well, it was supposed to be gum, but it was so hard to chew—and a small pack that consisted of four cigarettes. Again, it does not take a rocket scientist to figure out that these cigarettes have been in this box for over twenty years. Man, were these cigarettes strong, and because they were so dry, it didn't take long to smoke one of these cancer sticks. Then you had your P-38 can opener in each box. Anyway, you had to pack all these seven meals into your backpack. Then they would give each of us a bandana of sixty-millimeter machine-gun rounds, a pound of C-4, which is a plastic explosive, a LAW (light anti-armor weapon) rocket launcher, claymore mines, grenades, some pop-up flares, and then as much M16 ammunition that you could carry. All in all, you probably had a total of eighty to ninety pounds of gear that you were

responsible to carry. Now remember, all that we were issued were two—now hear me, two—canteens of water. Now that's two quarts of water. It's over one hundred degrees, you have all this shit to carry, and you have two quarts of water. Makes a lot of sense to me. Then the squad leader would tell us to saddle up. We're moving out. I felt like a mule with all this shit. Now things got interesting; where the hell are we going? Well, first, all platoons had turns taking point, taking the lead. All platoon squads took their turn at walking point and yap, it was our turn to walk point. Now being the FNG (new guy), I was the one who was told to take point. On top of everything that I already carried, they gave me a twelve-gauge shotgun and a machete. I had to cut a path, and Mack would keep me on a straight path using his map and compass to wherever we were going.

As I said, we moved in platoons, in a single file, and Bravo 1/3 Marines had three platoons plus a mortar platoon. Each platoon had four squads and a reinforced gun team. The point man was responsible to make sure that the path was big, wide, and safe enough so that everyone could go through. Now, do you think that I might have been a little bit timid about walking point? Hell, I just got here and now I was the point man. Shit, I was god damn petrified. Now, I've already heard of the horror stories of walking point, of running right into the enemy as you cut your path, of coming face-to-face with that guy named Charlie. You also had to worry about walking right into an ambush. This was a common occurrence while walking point, running right into an NVA ambush or a bunker complex. Being on the DMZ, we mainly dealt with the North Vietnamese Army (the NVA) and not with the Viet Cong, like they did in the Da Nang area. We had an organized army that we mostly had to deal with. The NVA was our enemy, and they were very sneaky. Another thing, who ever heard of a six-foot Vietnamese? Mostly, the Vietnamese were not much taller than five feet five. These six footers were actually Red Chinese soldiers working with the NVA. They all carried Russian AK-47s and Russian rocket launchers. Their machine guns and grenades were all from Red China. Hell, they even had tanks. It was our job to find these bastards and to kill them. Needless to say, the going was slow, and it was extremely hot. Not only did you have to be concerned about the enemy, you also had to be on the lookout for any natural obstacles, such as snakes and large man-eating animals. Vietnam was the home of many tigers, and these big cats were everywhere. I remember that the only thing that made us go off course were the snakes. Like I said, we had these cobras, and one time, the point man ran right into several cobras right on our path. We immediately detoured and cut a new trail around these snakes. Then there were the enemy bunker complexes. While you were humping, you didn't want to be walking point and stumbling onto one of these complexes. Another thing that the point man had to worry about was making sure that other marine units and air support knew that you were in the area. I remember that one time while walking point, I came face-to-face with that guy named Charlie. He looked like a little kid. I guess that he was walking point for his unit, and I was point for ours. We came face-to-face, looked at each other, and we both stopped. Neither one of us wanted anything to do with one another. He turned one way, and I turned the other. Our companies did finally get into a firefight because they were right parallel to us. We got into this firefight and wiped them all out. Finally, the word came down to recon the area and to stop and rest. Once this happened, it was someone else who would take point. It didn't take me long to figure out that there was no way that I was going to have enough water. I was already dehydrated and had heat stroke. So from that point on, I started collecting canteens anywhere and everywhere I could. Every time someone got wounded and would get medevaced out, I'd grab a couple of extra canteens. Now, at least I had four quarts of water on me. You know, it takes all kinds of people to be in 'Nam. You have the grunts, like me, who just want to do your time and make it out of there in one piece, and then you have your "John Wayne" types. These are usually a sergeant who was a seasoned vet and usually on his second or third tour in Vietnam. You couldn't miss them; they wore their hand grenades draping off their flak jackets, and many of them either carried an older M14 rifle or a Thompson machine gun. Every time that the shit hit the fan, they'd be up and running around, firing their rifle at the enemy, yelling and screaming, and they would actually run right at the oncoming enemy. I would think to myself, *How crazy are these bastards?* And for some reason, they would never get hit. Well, hardly ever. During this operation, which I later learned that we were on a search-and-destroy mission called Maine Crag, our point man walked us into two booby-trapped Chicom grenades. Four of the point team were wounded. They were eventually medevaced out to Quang Tri.

I didn't know it then, but we were actually patrolling the Laotian border. Whoever said that we were never in Cambodia or Laos were crazy. We did so many search-and-destroy missions in Laos and even into North Vietnam. Right now, we were part of Operation Main Craig, which, like I said, was on the Laotian border. We were ordered to conduct aggressive day and night patrols, set up ambushes, and cut off all trails that the NVA used to and from the border, as well as to stop the enemy from moving from the border onto Route 926, which was a major supply line for the NVA to the south.

Every night, we would set up, on some hill, a 360-degree perimeter and set up for the night. Each fire team dug foxholes, and we set up our field of fire, set up trip-wire booby traps and claymore mines and would set in for the night. The mortar company would be all set up behind us on the top of the hill. Then it was time to eat. Well, you know that pound of plastic explosives C-4? That is how we quickly heated up our food. Now, remember, this is an explosive and you have to know what you are doing. Remember that can of crackers that came in every carton of C rations? You open the can with your P-38 can opener and take the crackers out. Using your P-38 opener, you put several holes all around the outside of the can. This is very important because you have to make sure that you have plenty of oxygen so that the C-4 will burn and not blow up. Once the can is ready, you take a very small amount of C-4 and roll it into a small ball, about the size of a dime. You place this small amount of C-4 into the can. Open whatever you are going to warm up. You can even heat your water inside the canteen holder for your coffee or hot chocolate. Once you have whatever you're going to heat ready, take a match and light the C-4. Once lit, you will see a very white-hot ball of fire. Place whatever you are going to heat over the burning C-4. This will heat anything up so quickly. Never, ever try and put that ball of fire out. Never, ever stomp on it or put pressure on it. It will explode if not treated right. This is how we heated up our food, these stupid C rats.

I wrote home to all my family and asked them to start sending me care packages because these C rats were really giving me bad heartburn and diarrhea. Believe me, you did not want to get a bad case of diarrhea while in the bush. I think that you can use your own imagination and you'll know what I mean. It got so I hated to eat. So I started getting care packages of cans of tuna fish, spam, beef jerky, lots of Rolaids, and lots of presweetened Kool-Aid. The water was just as bad as the food and because sometimes we drank ground water we would get a bad case of diarrhea, and those halogen pills were real bitter. I remember that they made my pee green. Talk about going to relieve yourself while in the bush. It was easy to relieve yourself of urine but making a bowel movement was another thing. You could pee anywhere, but hopefully the old man would stop the column long enough so that you could go off the side of a trail, use your e-tool to dig a small hole, and then make your bowel movement in that hole. Now talk about how things could literally get real shitty, especially if you had a case of diarrhea.

Now, getting back to humping up these hills. We did this almost every day. I thought to myself that, hell, I wasn't in the United States Marine Corps, I was in the United States Mountain Climbing Club. It seemed that we were getting our share of the shits, if not more. For a while, we seemed to be getting hit almost every day. At the end of March, we had one of our patrols that got ambushed from a small bunker complex, and that same night, our perimeter was attacked. We suffered several WIA (wounded in action), but no one was mortally hit, and we did capture a lot of enemy firearms and explosives. The next morning, our wounded got medevaced out. The nighttime in Vietnam was so beautiful. I remember looking up at the sky and seeing all those stars, and it seemed that you could just reach out and touch one. When we had a full moon, it was like a grunt's reprieve. It was almost like daylight. Each night, a listening post would head out with their radio, and once in a while, we would send out an ambush patrol. This was a lot of fun. I remember going out on one of these LPs (listening posts), and the four of us went out alone, about five hundred feet in front of our lines. We had our Pric25 radio, and we just sat there all night and waited to see if any NVA were coming. God, I remember just hearing the freaking mosquitoes, and they were driving me crazy. I had a small tree between my legs so that I wouldn't roll down the hill. Then we heard noise coming from in front of us, and we just thought that the shit was going to hit the fan. Well, luckily, nothing happened on our LP, and morning came, and we made our way back to our lines.

A patrol, consisting of a platoon and a gun team would go out alone in the bush, set up along the side of the trail that we had made during the day or on a dry riverbed and just wait. Most of the time, nothing happened, but every once in a while, we would get a group of gooks sneaking around. We waited for them to get next to us, and we would open up on them, but most of the time, well, so far, we just sent out listening posts. Then you would hear the sounds of gunfire and explosions, and you'd see tracer rounds being fired out into the night. Our tracer rounds, which were one out of every five rounds, were red, and the enemy's tracer rounds were green. The reasoning behind these tracer rounds was so that you knew the direction of where you were shooting. And every time you saw this, you knew that one of your sister companies was being hit by Charlie. You would just thank God that it wasn't you.

During the night, your mind would play games with you, and you would hear everything including those stupid lizards calling you names. You swore that Charlie was sneaking up on you. Then someone would just say, "No, it's probably just a rock ape." You stayed up all night long waiting for Charlie to come at you.

Morning would come, and we would be told to saddle up. We would be on the move in ten. You had ten minutes to eat and to get all your stuff together, and then we would move out to another hilltop. About every seven days or so, a chopper would come in and resupply us with food, water, and ammunition and if you were lucky, they would also bring in the mail. Getting your mail was a real treat because it brought you back to your loved ones, back home to the World. As the days went by, everything seemed to get much more carefree. I really didn't care anymore and wasn't worried about Charlie like when I first arrived in country. As weeks went by, I wasn't the FNG anymore. We would be in the same clothes every day and night, and because of the extreme heat, your clothes would start to rot, especially in your crotch area. We didn't have a chance to wash up, other than brushing our teeth, and we all smelled bad, but that was all right because we all smelled the same way. We were not allowed to use deodorants or anything because if we did, the NVA soldiers would be able to smell us. God knows that you knew when they were around or close-by because we could smell them. And like I said, it didn't take long that I wasn't the new guy anymore. Marines would get medevaced out almost every day for whatever reason—sickness, heat exhaustion, jungle rot, malaria, being wounded by shrapnel, or whatever. Remember that John Wayne-syndrome marine? Well, one time we were all humping up a hill, and all of a sudden, we heard a loud explosion. Then the word comes down, two wounded and one dead. You think to yourself, *What the fuck happened?* Well, I'll tell you what happened; that "John Wayne" idiot was walking through the bush, and one of the pins on his hand grenade that was hanging from his flak jacket got caught on a branch, and the pin came out. Next thing, *boom!* Now he got blown up, and when he did, the rest of his grenades went off, and two marines in front of him got wounded by flying shrapnel from the grenades. This is why so many things happen so quickly in the bush. At the beginning of April, which now we were on an operation called Virginia Ridge, our point man walked right into an ambush. This marine did not get hit by the enemy, but he received a fatal wound by one of our own marines. We appeared to have several more of these incidents, and we were losing marines every day. Because of this, you made rank quickly in Nam and now I was promoted, a field promotion, to Lance/Corporal. Now I was the assistant squad leader, and I now carried an M-79 grenade launcher and a forty-five-caliber pistol. I was the second man in charge of our squad. Now, the M-79 is quite a weapon, and I loved it. It had this distinct sound when fired. Mostly I used HE rounds, which are similar to a grenade. When fired, it made a *bloop* sound. It was great. Then for close range, I had a large shotgun-type round that was full of small dart-type rounds called fléchette rounds, which had approximately forty-five small darts in a plastic casing. The M-79 could also fire smoke grenades, CS gas, and flares.

After humping for days and searching for any Viet Cong, rice caches (we knew that if we found these types of supplies, these people were actually VC) and were hiding and storing these supplies for the NVA, who were coming down from the north. Therefore, every vill that we came upon, we thoroughly searched, and if these supplies were found, we would totally destroy the vill, weapons, and ammunition in villages that we passed through. We walked through rice paddies, and everywhere we looked, we saw Vietnamese kids with their big-ass water buffalos walking along paths, and then we would see Vietnamese men and women wearing black pajamas. These people were known as

Montagnard, which was French for "mountain people." They were the residents of the villages, and most were sympathetic toward the North Vietnamese and were part of the Viet Cong. Now, these rice paddies, no one ever told me that once you walk in a rice paddy you are supposed to stop once you got out of the water and check your ankles and feet. We would stop because first off, we've been walking in water. We would take our boots off, and guess what? We would be covered in bloodsuckers. Well, the first time this happened, it freaked me out, but after a while of doing this, it was just second nature to check your feet for bloodsuckers, and while we are on the subject of feet, my feet seemed to be always wet. I couldn't keep them dry to save my life. Therefore, after a while, you developed what they called trench foot. Now this was not good. Layers of skin would just peel off from the bottom of your feet. Your feet became raw and hurt and swelled up. Again, no one told you about this possibly happening. No one prepared us for this. Now in my letters home, I asked that they also send me some type of odorless foot powder.

One afternoon we walked right into a makeshift village, which was comprised of fourteen thatched huts with two pigpens and a few chicken coops. We also found nine recently built bunkers with bamboo matting floors. No one was around other than a few pigs and some chickens. We knew that the NVA had just been here. We searched the area and found an NVA poncho, AK-47 ammunition, machetes, an NVA belt and shoulder patch, tools, canteens, and cooking utensils. We destroyed the huts and blew up all the bunkers. We could feel that Charlie wasn't far off at all. We continued to search the whole area, and nothing else was located. We called in an air strike in the area.

Now let me say this about these air strikes. Sometimes, whoever called in the coordinates for these strikes gave the wrong information, and I can tell you that many times these air strikes came so close to us that you swear these assholes in the rear of our artillery bases on these bomb runs were trying to hit us. You could hear the shrapnel flying all around. I thanked God that they were not using Willie Peter (white phosphorus) rounds. Again, this was friendly fire that we had to contend with.

We then reached Hill 55, and we set in for five days. During this time, we got resupplied, and new recruits were choppered in as replacements. We set out nightly patrols and ambush squads, but we did not encounter the enemy during this time. Finally, we secured the

hill and were airlifted to the area of the Rockpile in Dong Ha Valley
and stayed there until the end of the month. Once your company gets
back to a firebase, you would hear all kinds of horror stories. One
story that went around really quickly was that our sister company,
Charlie Company, was on patrol, and the point team observed
four male subjects in the bush. Three of these males appeared to be
Orientals, but the fourth was a white male with blond hair and a blond
beard. This same individual was wearing a marine cover, green pants,
and a large wide black leather belt with a bright-red cloth hanging
from the left side of the belt. The fire team did not fire on these
four due to the fact that they were possibly friendlies in the area. So
Charlie Company pulled back and reported what they observed to the
company commander. The company commander checked it out with
HQ, and they advised that there were no friendlies in that area. So now,
we possibly had a rogue marine on the enemy's side. Well, that was
great news to hear. While in the area, we continued to go out on patrol,
looking for any signs of the enemy. Then, just like that, the word
came down that we were going to be choppered out for a three-day
in-country R&R (rest and recreation). They loaded us up on choppers,
and we went to a place called China Beach, which was on the ocean
just southeast of Da Nang. Man, was that a beautiful beach. You would

never know that there was a war going on anywhere. This place was highly fortified, and we were able to go swimming, eat hot meals, have hot showers, get resupplied with all new clothing, and have all the beer we could drink. It was great. They took all our weapons and ammunition and any explosives and placed them all in one tent. The old man didn't want anyone to get liquored up and start a firefight. He wanted to make sure that the blacks and the whites didn't get into it. We even had these concerts that were put on by these groups. It was a USO-sponsored show, but the girls dancing were all gooks, no round eyes at all. It was pretty good anyway. Then one afternoon, we

had the treat of our life. A USO show that was all Australian girls with long blond hair and round eyes. Man, what any one of us would have given just to spend a minute alone with any of these girls. They wore these skimpy two-piece outfits all trimmed in lace. You didn't want it to end, but like all good things, it did come to an end. The word came down that we were going on another operation. We were all issued new clothing and re-supplied with C rations, water and ammunition. They loaded us up and choppered us back to the Rockpile for another mission.

At the beginning of May, the word came down that we would be involved again in another search-and-destroy mission called Pink Panther and would involve the Route 9 area in Quang Tri Province up to the Laotian border. Now who said that we did not cross over to Laos? Well, guess what? We crossed the border several times going after the NVA as they tried to retreat to the east into Laos. We patrolled the Ben Hoi riverside and conducted several ambushes on the North Vietnamese Army. We finally reached Vandegrift Firebase, and while at the firebase, we experienced another accidental detonation of a hand grenade, which killed one marine and wounded three others. Another stupid, needless mistake by, again, one of those John Wayne-type marines. Then while on a break, this fucking idiot marine tripped or whatever and accidentally shot another marine in the head. I thought to myself, *What the hell is going on?* Another friendly-fire death. How stupid can one be? The company was pretty well tired and frustrated, and they ordered us to stand down for a while. We ended up doing perimeter detail for the Seabees at the KK Bridge, along Route 9 near the Washout. Now this was a good assignment. We set up a perimeter around the Seabees compound and around their work sites. They were rebuilding the bridge, and they needed fire support. Now let me tell you, these guys know how

to make a bad situation good. Remember, these are the Navy Seabees. They have everything, and if they don't have it, they'll make it. Hell, we even had hot food, hot showers, and all. Every morning the Seabees had an ordinance patrol go out and clear the road of any enemy land mines. They even had a tank platoon to assist them along the roadway. These guys knew how to make things happen. We stayed there with them for about two weeks and then got relieved because we got orders to conduct another sweep and continue with operation Virginia Ridge.

Morning came, and we packed up and took off again for another search-and-destroy mission, Virginia Ridge, which involved patrolling along the DMZ. We started climbing all the hills and mountains again, setting up night patrols and going from one place to another. We kept heading north and moving at a pretty good clip and making good time. We had a few skirmishes, ran into an abandoned enemy bunker complex, searched villages, but there were no causalities other than the normal heat strokes, jungle rot, malaria, and everything this crazy country dished out. If it wasn't one thing, it was another. Humping up on the side of one hill to just hump down the side of another, until we reached wherever we were ordered to go, always humping through those stupid mountains, looking for that guy named Charlie. It got really hot, and we were moving slowly. We were stopping about every half hour because of the intense heat. Even veteran marines who have been in the bush a long time were having a hard time making the hump. It was fucking unbearably hot. One of the hills that we climbed and humped over was wet, and we had the hardest time getting up over that hill. We would start humping and then we would slide down because of the mud. What a mess, and we were all covered in mud. It was so discouraging, and the commanding officer, our captain, who we called the Old Man or Six, was getting so frustrated and upset because we couldn't move quickly enough.

Well, let me tell you, I was never so relieved to finally reached Con Thien Firebase. We were deployed to take over the defense and perimeter of the base, which was right on the DMZ. Con Thien translated into "hill of angels." Well, this was not heaven, I'll tell you that. Now remember, these firebases like Con Thien were made by the French Foreign Legion. Remember I told you that Vietnam was originally a French colony and they had control of the country. That meant that the bunkers that we were in were old. There were rats, bugs, big-ass spiders, and scorpions all over the place. More shit to worry about, getting bitten by one of these bastards. At night, we would send out listening posts, which consisted of four marines equipped with a field radio, and their job was to stay out about three hundred meters or so in front of our perimeter and just listen to see if they hear the enemy approaching us during the night. Once at Con Thien, we were able to see a glimpse of a North Vietnamese army base off in the distance in North Vietnam, and every day, that base would fire rockets at our position and we would fire back. We had these tracked armored vehicles that were called Ontos, and they had six 106-millimeter recoilless rifles on them. These bastards were real accurate and bad. Then we had these Dusters that were also tracked armored vehicles, like a small tank, that had twin forty-millimeter guns and a fifty-caliber machine gun. We had several Ontoses and Dusters around the perimeter, and we also had four-wheel open vehicles called the Mule that were equipped with one 106 rifle around the base, and these bad boys would work out every night, firing out into the darkness toward the DMZ. This went on every day and night. We stayed at Con Thien for two weeks, and we were getting pretty comfortable there. One morning, Mack asked the Old Man if he could take a reinforced squad into the DMZ, and the Old Man gave Mack the OK, so we loaded up our squad of nine marines, a four-man gun team, and a corpsman, which made us a reinforced squad, and we left on patrol into the DMZ and right into North Vietnam. Now we didn't see any NVA soldiers, but we did locate a major trail that they used, and we saw several areas that had some remains of where the NVA had been, like old tennis-type shoes, empty cans of food, fire pits, a little rice here and there. We figured that we were on one of the NVA's resupply trails. We radioed back to the Old Man and advised what we had located, and he told us to continue for a few more meters and then start heading back. We continued, but we still didn't find any NVA solders. As we were patrolling in a section of North Vietnam, I saw a piece of paper that was on the ground. This paper, which was about three by six inches, had Vietnamese writing on both sides. I suspected

CŨNG CÁC CÁN-BINH BẮC-VIỆT.

Một trong những mối bận tâm lớn nhất của các cấp chỉ-huy của bạn là tìm hết cách để che đậy sự thật.

Thư từ giữa các bạn và gia-đình bị kiểm duyệt gắt gao và hạn chế đến mức hầu như cắt đứt mọi liên hệ với gia-đình.

Các bạn không được tự-do nghe các đài phát thanh và đọc truyền đơn Quốc-Gia để đối chiếu với thực tế mà tìm ra sự thật. Các bạn chỉ được tuyên truyền theo luận điệu một chiều vô cùng nhàm tai.

7 - 321 - 69

Lúc ở Bắc cán bộ đảng phỉnh phờ các bạn rằng vào Nam để tiếp thu, chẳng cần phải đánh đá nhiều vì đã giải phóng 2/3 dân số, kiểm soát 3/4 đất đai. Nhưng cớ sao các bạn lại phải trốn chui nhủi ở các vùng rừng núi.

Cho dù các bạn chịu đựng nổi sự vô ơn bạc nghĩa của đảng một khi bạn thành thần tàn ma dại. Các thương binh sống dở chết dở mà đảng cố tình bỏ quên sẽ là hình ảnh của bạn mỗi ngày gần đây.

Vậy từ nay hễ ai lần la tuyên truyền với bạn " Trường kỳ gian khổ" hoặc " Càng gần chiến. thắng, càng nhiều gian nan" thì các bạn có quyền mỉm cười hoài nghi.

that it was a piece of our propaganda program that the United States used against the NVA. You see, the US had several of these propaganda campaigns going all over the I-Corps area, and this was one of them. I took this paper and I put it carefully in my pocket. I eventually got this paper translated into English, and this is what it said,

To servicemen of North Vietnam:

One of the main worries of your commanders is to hide the truth by any means.

Your correspondence with friends and relatives is strictly censored and limited up to losing any contact with families.

You are not allowed to listen to the radio stations and read government leaflets where you could discover the truth.

You are propagandized obtrusively by one-sided point of view only.

7-321-69

In the North, the party leaders coaxed you to going to the south just to take over without serious fighting, because 2/3 of its population had been freed and 3/4 of the territory was under their control. However, why do you have to hide and slink in jungle areas?

Though you are tolerating such ingratitude of the party, once you will be a walking corpse. Your destiny in the nearest future is to become a miserable disabled soldier, which is intentionally forgotten by the party.

From now on, if anybody agitates for "Long privations" or "The closer our victory, the more sufferings there are," you have the right to smile skeptically.

We searched the area for more evidence of the NVA, but nothing further was located, so we started back south to Con Thien.

We finally got back to base, and we learned that a chopper had come in with new supplies. We even got new camouflage fatigues, a resupply of socks and mail. Remember that three beer thing, well, they even brought us in a pallet of beer. It was real skunk piss, Black Label beer, but it was beer. Then one morning, just like that, the word came out that we were going to be leaving. We were going to be relieved by another company. Again, we loaded up with our seven meals, water, and all our ammunition that we could carry—our LAW rockets and hand grenades. Once our replacements were set in, we set out into the bush. We were told that we would probably be out in the bush for months on the same search-and-destroy mission. That's all we ever did; we went out on these campaigns of search and destroy. We kept looking for the enemy, their bunkers, their underground hospitals, and rice and weapons stashes. And all the time, we had air and artillery support dropping their bombs and napalm bombs on all sides of us as we humped through the hills, up over Dong Ha mountain to Camp Carroll and back through Dong Ha Valley over to Razor Back, the Rockpile, and over to the Cam Lo area. We walked everywhere, and once in a while, we would encounter the enemy, but mostly, we had to fight nature's elements, such as the heat, bugs, snakes, and then monsoons.

Now, let me explain something. You think you've seen rain? You have never experienced rain until you experienced the monsoon rains. Once it starts to rain, you would swear to God that it seemed it will never end. And anyone who thinks that there are no bugs or mosquitoes when it rains hard, you're out of your head. During the monsoons, the mosquitoes seemed to be bigger and worse. All you could do was to keep your poncho over your head all the time, even when we humped through the bush. We kept going as if nothing was going on at all. The temperature would drop down to about eighty-five degrees, and you would swear that you were freezing to death because you were always soaked and wet, but we kept going. Several marines caught malaria really bad, but they couldn't get medevaced out because choppers could not land due to the heavy rains. Finally, as quick as the rain started, it stopped. Now we humped in the mud. There were streams everywhere and rivers were flooded, but that didn't stop us. We only stopped at the end of the day to set up our defensive perimeter, dig a so-called foxhole, and lie in the mud. We would make a temporary LZ (landing zone) so that we could get supplies and get our sick medevaced out.

The month of May 1969 was real rough. We were still on the same search-and-destroy mission of Operation Virginia Ridge. We were phasing out of Operation Maine Crag and redeployed north toward the DMZ and Route 9, to locate and destroy enemy forces infiltrating across the D. Our command ordered us to use small groups, two and three squads of marines, to patrol the area and try and get the NVA on the run. We were like hit-and-run squads, and it was very effective. The heat was just unbelievable, and we were having so many heat casualties. We humped every day from one hill to another. A couple of times we would start to set in, clear a field of fire, dig a foxhole, and start clearing for a landing zone, and then just like that, we would get the word that we were moving out to another location. All that fucking work for nothing. It didn't make any sense at all. One time we moved out after digging and clearing, and Charlie Company took our hill that we just cleared. During the night, we watched as that company got hit. Tracer rounds were flying everywhere. They called in Puff the Magic Dragon to assist the company. Puff was a modified AC 47 double-prop airplane that had three 7.62-mm Gatling guns. Each gun was capable of shooting six thousand rounds per minute—that's right, one hundred rounds a second—for a full output of eighteen thousand rounds per minute. Puff could clear a football field in about thirty seconds. When Puff fired, all you saw was a steady stream of red tracers. It was amazing to watch as Puff worked on these gooks. When Puff was there, you knew that the shit was really hitting the fan. The gooks were trying to infiltrate their position and were really giving them a beating. I guess that the old saying is right when they say that things happen for a reason. Well, the old man upstairs was watching over us. It just was meant to be that we moved from that hill. The next morning we sent a platoon to check on Charlie Company. They got hit two days in a row, and they had several casualties. We were about two hundred meters from the DMZ, and the NVA seemed to be everywhere. We headed out slowly, and then our point man heard some noise. Next thing we knew, NVA regulars were right in front of us. We set up a platoon-size ambush. There had to be a whole column of NVA, and we fired on them as they walked by. Man, were they surprised. They ran everywhere, trying to get away from us. We radioed back to our company, and then the mortar platoon fired on them, and they saturated the area around our ambush. After the firing stopped, we were ordered to recon and mop up the area for any more NVA. We slowly walked the area and located a bunker complex. Well, let me tell you about these bunker complexes. The NVA used these bunkers as their entrances to the tunnels that they dug. In these tunnels, the gooks would set up underground makeshift hospitals, living areas, and ammunition and food storage. So now, it was up to one of our so-called tunnel rats to go into these tunnels and check it out for any signs of the enemy. A tunnel rat was usually one of our smaller and shorter grunts within the company. We had several designated tunnel rats in our company, and we had two in our platoon. These guys had balls because all they would have was a flashlight and a forty-five-caliber pistol. Our tunnel rat located a hospital and all kinds of rice and ammunition, including grenades and rocket launchers. We gathered up all this stuff and then blew the complex up. We located all kinds of AK-47 rifles and more ammunition. There were several dead NVA soldiers, and we searched all of them for so-called souvenirs. I grabbed an NVA officer's belt, which had a silver-colored star on the buckle, and I also took his Russian revolver, a Chinese-made knife, and his helmet. Everyone was grabbing up what they could. We did well, and the Old Man was happy about our find. We finally reached Charlie Company, and they were happy to finally see friendly faces. They had been hit hard, and we stayed there for about three hours, helping them get their dead and wounded out on choppers. At the same time, command back in Quang Tri choppered out new replacements for Charlie Company. Once these new guys came in, we were ordered to move out and hump our way back to our hill.

Now it was the nineteenth of May 1969. It was Ho Chi Minh's birthday. It was commonly known that the NVA forces had a habit of launching major attacks on national holidays, like Tet or birthdays of historical figures. So the Old Man figured that we better get reinforced and dig in good for any surprise attacks; after all, it was Ho's birthday. We set up a reinforced perimeter around our hill. Command even sent in two tanks. Now let me tell you, tanks do not maneuver well in the bush. One tank was coming in to set up within our perimeter and while it was coming in, it hit a booby-trap land mine and that mine blew one of the tracks off of the tank. Now we have this disabled tank to deal

with. Luckily, the night was quiet, and we didn't hear or see anything. That next morning, we were ordered to move out but before we did, we waited around until Command could send in another tank to tow the disabled tank out. We were to hump to a hill that was about two hundred meters from the DMZ. Now let me tell you what, we were now right in the gooks' territory. This was their backyard, and we were there to play. Being this close also meant that we were now right in range for the NVA's eighty-two-millimeter mortars and their rockets. We reached our hill, Hill 130, and were ordered to dig in good. Then choppers came in with more food, water, ammunition, and mail. One chopper brought in two more mortar crews to set up. This meant that we were going to stay here for a little while. A three-squad ambush team was sent out to set up along a streambed at the bottom of our hill. Well, just like the Old Man figured, the ambush team observed a full platoon of NVA regulars moving about in a single line along the other side of the stream. The ambush team actually was watching as a full platoon-size group of NVA were heading toward the rest of our company on Hill 130. The Old Man was notified, and he told the ambush team to let at last half of these NVA soldiers go by and then open up on them and give them everything they had. The Old Man put the rest of the company on high alert and ordered that the mortar platoon get all their tubes ready to fire. The captain then gave the order for the mortars to fire, and the ambush team walked the mortars right into the enemy's position. Gooks were running everywhere, and the ambush team fired on them as they were trying to escape the mortars. Then all shit hit the fan. We had heavy artillery called in, and I had never seen so many bomb strikes come in so fast. We even had air strikes from the USS *New Jersey*'s sixteen-inch guns. For once in a long while, we really had these gooks on the run, and they were dropping like flies. Puff was called in to finish off any of the gooks who were trying to survive. For over five hours, the shooting and bombing continued, and we just saturated the entire area. We had no casualties. It was unbelievable, not one of our grunts got even a scratch. It was great. As morning came, the Old Man took our platoon down to the ambush site to do an estimate and mop-up. Gooks were lying everywhere, limbs torn from their bodies from all the bombs and explosions. During the mop-up, we located several wounded gooks, and the word came down—take no prisoners. It was like a turkey shoot. There was no *Chu Hoi* this morning. By the way, *Chu Hoi* means "I give up, I surrender" in Vietnamese, and at the beginning of each major operation, our choppers would drop these white flyers that were explaining to the gooks what the Chu Hoi Program was all about. We would find these flyers all over the place as we humped from hill to hill. Anyway, as I said, no *Chu Hoi* today. These slant-eyed bastards did not have a chance. More gook souvenirs, trophies if you wish, for all the grunts who were involved with the mop-up and ambush. I watched as one grunt next to me walked up to a gook, who had his hand up and was mumbling "*Chu Hoi, Chu Hoi*," and the grunt shot this gook right in the head. Mack simply looked at me and said, "No fucking *Chu Hoi* today, you dead bastard." I'll never forget that day. It was my twentieth birthday, May 22, 1969. Then I saw a marine from first squad, and he was cutting a dead NVA's head off with his KA-BAR. This marine placed that head in a claymore bag and later boiled that head into just a skeleton and mounted that skeleton head onto the top of a wooden walking stick. The first ten hours of this day will be etched in my mind forever. I'll never forget the look on that gook's face just before having the top of his head shot off.

The rest of the morning remained quiet, and the Old Man was really in his glory because he had a big body count to radio back to battalion. Choppers were called in, and all kinds of NVA supplies were choppered back to headquarters in Quang Tri. At the same time, we received a resupply of ammunition. But no water came. What's up with that? Where's the fucking water? The Old Man got on the horn and asked where our supply of water was. Somebody obviously fucked up big time. There were a lot of fuckups in 'Nam. If it wasn't one thing, it was another.

It appeared as though we lost more marines to friendly fire than anything else—air support dropping a bomb too near our position, a mistake in coordinates while calling in an air strike. The John Wayne syndrome that I mentioned earlier—some marine trying to be a hard-ass, a hero, and all they did was put everyone around them in danger. One excuse after another, and everything, I am sure, was attributed to KIA (killed in action) or MIA (missing in action) or WIA (wounded in action). Never that it was friendly fire. I'll get back to that in a few minutes.

It was very hot and very humid. Everyone was running low on water. We were on one of these so-called search-and-destroy missions, and at that time, we barely had any water. Choppers could not get in to us to resupply us with water, for whatever reason. The water situation was so bad that we started drinking our own sweat. We were sent out again to recon an area and assist our sister company, Charlie Company, who had received numerous casualties during a nighttime firefight. We were scouting out the area around the other side of our Hill 130, looking for KIA and WIA marines who had been left behind. Charlie Company broke the golden rule. Marines were always taught to never leave or abandon his fellow marine no matter what. The dead and wounded were never left alone. No one was supposed to be left behind.

The hill next to Hill 130, where Charlie Company was supposed to set in, was a large NVA (North Vietnamese Army) bunker complex. We were tasked with recon in the area, to seek and destroy any enemy, and to recover our fellow fallen marines from Charlie Company. We did locate several KIA marines, and I remember checking their vital signs for any signs of life at all. Once not receiving any pulse, I checked their canteens to see if they had any water. If they did, I took their canteens. I don't know if anyone else ever felt the feeling of needing to drink water but couldn't because you didn't have any water to drink. I had a total of eight canteens now, and I vowed that I would never run out of water again. At the same time, we cleared all the enemy bunkers and set explosives and blew them all up. We carried these dead marines to a makeshift LZ and waited for choppers to come in and carry these marines back to the rear. This took us all afternoon to do, and we worked very slowly and cautiously as we checked out the entire hillside to make sure that we didn't get blown up by any booby traps. During this same time frame, we would recon Hill 174 and fill our canteens with any water that we could find, including any running water along the ground. We filled our canteens and used several halogen pills to attempt to purify the water. This was not the first time that we were forced to drink water from rivers and streams that ran through the I Corps area of South Vietnam.

A few days later, on May 25, 1969, our company was tasked with a special operation called Centerpede. While we were holding a defensive position, we set in just southeast of Cam Lo. At about 1745 hours, I was sitting on the side of my foxhole and just started eating some C rations. We had arrived here earlier in the afternoon and were dug in for the night. It was very hot, and all I had on was a green T-shirt and my unzipped flak jacket, when there was a huge explosion that went off behind our position, near the top of the hill. This explosion was so loud and powerful that the force knocked me and several other marines around me forward into our foxholes. The explosion was so forceful that I lost a partial denture: six (6) teeth, three (3) on each side of this partial that was made for me while I was in boot camp at Parris Island. As the force of the explosion made me hit the front wall of our foxhole, the force just threw this partial out of my mouth. I never recovered that partial. All I remember hearing was loud ringing in my ears. Then there were several other explosions that continued behind us for quite some time. It was complete chaos, and everyone had no idea where these explosives were coming from or what caused them. All we knew was that we had a large fire that was making these mortar rounds go off. What happened was that a pallet of eighty-one mortars went off. As a result of the fire, cook-off rounds continued to explode, and there was debris and shrapnel flying all over.

I suffered a scratch on my right arm, just above my elbow. This scratch was not severe enough for me to be medevaced, so I remained in the bush. As a result of these explosions and cook-off rounds, several marines, approximately fifteen (15) marines, from Bravo 1/3 were fatally wounded. Two (2) of these marines' bodies were never found due to the severity of the initial huge explosion that went off. Several others, including myself, received injuries from these explosions. I recall looking over to my right, approximately two (2) foxholes over, and observed another marine slumped over, leaning forward facedown over the edge of the front of his foxhole. I made my way toward him and pulled him back into the foxhole. I did not observe any visible marks on this marine, but he was lifeless with his eyes wide open. I yelled for a corpsman, and when the corpsman reached us, he simply closed the marine's eyes with his fingers and went on. We later carried that marine in a poncho liner to a makeshift landing zone, and he was medevaced out. I never forgot the look on that marine's face. There was no blood, no visible wounds. He appeared to be just sleeping. I later learned that this marine was struck behind his right ear with a small piece of shrapnel and that the shrapnel lodged inside of the marine's head, in his brain. To this day, I can still see that marine's face. This is why I said that I saw more of my fellow marines who died needlessly. You can bet that these marines who were mortally wounded were all classified as KIA (killed in action), when in fact, it was because of an idiot from the mortar company who caused these marines to die. What happened was that fucking nut was leaning up against a pallet of mortar rounds, cooking his meal and using C-4 to heat-up his C-rats and he either used too much C-4 or whatever, he did something wrong. A fire started within the mortar pit and he tried to put that fire out. The fire quickly got out of control and mortar rounds started to go off. What a fucking mess! Needless to say, that same marine's body was never recovered. He literally was blown to bits. Once things calmed down, our head navy corpsman, Doc Sloan, gave me antibiotics in the form of penicillin to assist in fighting off any infection to my arm. That didn't last long. I remained in the bush, and the doc continued to give me antibiotics to help fight off the infection. Eventually, over the weeks that followed, the infection caused my arm to swell up, and jungle rot, cellulitis, set in. I sustained a very bad infection, which caused my entire arm and right hand to swell up to about three times the normal size, with fluid along with a fever that was so obvious Doc Sloan ordered me to get on the next chopper to be medevaced back to Quang Tri so that I could receive the proper medical attention. While waiting for the right time to be choppered out, the company continued to push forward up a ridge. My right hand and arm were pretty much useless due to the pain and swelling.

During this push, a booby-trap tree mine was tripped. I think I was the one who tripped it, but I really don't know for sure. All I remember is that I saw the black comm wire that was lying on the path, and the next thing I knew, I heard a loud explosion. I know that I sustained the full back blast and the force of this explosion, and it literally threw me off to the right side of the trail, approximately ten (10) to twenty (20) feet into a pile of brush. I remember that I could not feel my legs, which were under my torso, and my ears were ringing so loudly that I could not hear anything other than that ringing in my ears. Two marines right behind me sustained shrapnel injury, and they were eventually medevaced out to Quang Tri. One of these injured marines said that he had the million-dollar wound, as a piece of shrapnel metal went through his jungle boot right into his ankle.

I got on the next chopper and also landed in Quang Tri, where they operated on my arm just above my right elbow, which was where the initial scratch occurred on May 25, 1969, in the Quang Tri Field Hospital. They kept up daily treatment of reopening the wound and draining all the fluids out of my hand, fingers, and right arm. Man, did that hurt. They first cut my arm open to my elbow bone, and they cleaned it out and started to drain it. I remember that the smell of that fluid was awful. They scraped it and packed it, no stitches at all, and every day, they would take out the packing that they put into the wound the day before. Man, that felt like they were ripping my arm open all over again. They would squeeze the fluid out, inch by inch, to the center of my arm, and squeeze that fluid out through the hole in my arm. Then they would repack the wound. They did the same thing each day until all the fluid was gone. Now it was time for my arm to heal.

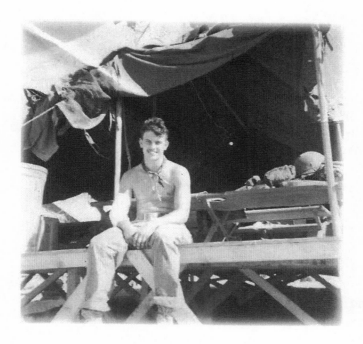

After about three (3) weeks, I was returned to light duty within headquarters at Quang Tri.

While in the field hospital, the base commander would visit the hospital and talk to the wounded marines. On this one morning, the commander came over to my cot and presented me with a Purple Heart. To this day, I have that Purple Heart and the original case he gave it to me in.

I eventually returned to the bush a few weeks later and rejoined the company at the Cam Lo Bridge, near the Washout in Dong Ha Valley. We were back doing perimeter defense for the Seabees. I didn't care because, again, we at least ate hot meals and had cold beer. My squad had a 106-mm recoilless rifle, which is actually an antitank weapon, mounted near our bunker. I guess that now, at night, the NVA

was coming down from the north on Route 9 and placing land mines all along the road by the bridge that the Seabees were working on. Every morning, a patrol would go out with mine detectors and clear the road. We even had our own tanks patrolling along the road, and I would watch as they would use their flamethrowers to set fire to all the brush along the side of the road. This continued every morning while we were there. We never did get to fire that 106. It just stayed right there on a large tripod in front of our foxhole in plain sight. I don't know, but maybe it was there to show the gooks that we had heavy and long-range weapons in place. Who knows? All I know is that these types of weapons were not there when we first arrived at the bridge a few months back.

It was the end of May, and we were told to pack up our gear and get ready to move out soon. Mack was getting short, which meant that his time in Vietnam was almost over, and he was going to rotate back to the World, and now I was starting to take over our squad. We had some FNGs come in, and I assigned them to fill in different fire team positions in our squad. When a new guy comes into the squad, the squad leader would interview that marine, and we would write down in our notebook certain pertinent information, like his full name, rank, date of birth, service number, date he came in the country, home address, and next of kin. We asked for his blood type, his boot size, what he had for a weapon, his serial number, and his religion. We would go over all his gear, and then I'd make suggestions of what to discard because it would have no use in the field. These items, like any unnecessary gear, would just add to the weight of what he had to hump. These were items like too many bars of soap, aftershave, bottles of vitamins, too much writing material, gas masks, and any other items that he could discard.

Let me tell you about writing home. I was in 'Nam some three months now, and I developed a very bad attitude. I wasn't writing home because I really didn't have much to say. Hell, they wouldn't understand what I was going through anyway. In the short time that I've been in Nam, I had seen so much death that I just became like a zombie. I did not give a shit about too much. Anyway, my mom, back in the World, got upset and worried about me, so she asked my dad to reach out to the local Red Cross and asked if they could check on me. They finally caught up with me, and my CO, Captain Dan, sent for me and asked why I wasn't writing home. I guess that I just looked at him. The next thing he told me was that we had enough shit to put up with out here in the bush without the goddamn Red Cross on his ass because one of his men wasn't writing home. He basically ordered me to take care of this, and that he didn't want to hear from the Red Cross again. Anyway, I think you get the picture, and yes, I started writing home more often.

There's another thing I would like to mention. You know there were a lot of stories about the American soldiers in Vietnam mutilating the dead NVA or VC bodies by cutting off their ears and then carrying these ears or whatever on their belts or hanging them on a string. I can assure you that we did not do this at all. Other than having that skeleton head mounted on a walking stick, we did not take part in that ear stuff. We all carried the ace of spades, and mine was on my helmet. Why the ace of spades? Well, that card was known as the Card of Death. The Death Card, the ace of spades, was considered bad luck by

the Viet Cong and the North Vietnamese Army (NVA). We all carried that card, and like me, most of us had it attached to the front of our helmet. I had my ace of spades given to me by Mack, my squad leader, when I first came to the squad back in March. I had several of these cards, ace of spades, now with me in my pack. As for the skeleton head, each one of our platoons would take turns carrying that walking stick as we humped through the bush. It was kind of like our mascot. I told you, war has a way of making you do crazy things. After a while, you didn't even give a shit if you got wounded. It just didn't matter anymore. 'Nam made you just not care what happened, because you knew that, at any moment, Charlie could be right out there to get you.

Word came down that we were going to be humping our way back to Con Thien and along the DMZ. Our orders were to get to the DMZ area, set up squad-size patrols, and support recon patrols in and along the D. Then if the shit hit the fan, we would be reinforced by a platoon-size reaction force to assist in destroying the enemy. Shit, it felt like we just came from there. The Old Man said that we had received information from intelligence that numerous sightings of the enemy were made, and it appeared that the Twenty-Seventh NVA Regiment was moving south, toward the lowlands, and we were tasked with trying to stop them by any means possible. Operation Virginia Ridge was back on. During this phase of the operation, which was a search-and-destroy operation in the Cam Lo, Huong Hoa, and Gio Linh area of Quang Tri Province into the DMZ, we again were operating under new tactical orders to use platoon-size or smaller patrols moving out at least every twenty-four hours or less. This tactic was to keep everyone on the move and attempt to confuse the NVA. We also received word that intelligence had information that the NVA was using their Twenty-Fourth Sapper Company in and around the D and the lowlands. A sapper company was about two to three hundred gooks (NVA). They would tie off their feet at the ankles and their wrists and, basically, were suicide fighters. They would hit our lines with rocket launchers and satchel charges, walk over any concertina wire, which was like razor blades, and were ready to give up their lives to kill us. We also had reports that the Fourth and Fifth Battalions of the Eighty-Eighth NVA Regiment were also in the vicinity of the D. Let me tell you, that's a hell of a lot of goddamn gooks! Anyway, on May 30, we set out, but before heading out, we were resupplied with seven (7) days of C rations, all the ammunition you could carry, grenades, LAW rocket launchers, claymore mines, M-60 ammo for the gun teams, C-4, and this time, we were also issued our own body bags. Now that was a real morale booster. Imagine what was going on in our heads—we carried our own body bags just in case we were fatally wounded. What a thought. These bags were black plastic-type bags with a long zipper. It was like carrying our own coffin. Our platoon was the lead platoon, and my squad was point squad. I had to pick someone to walk point man, and I picked an FNG but his fire team leader said that he wanted to take the point. We headed north, down on Dong Ha Valley toward the DMZ. We humped along the lowlands, along the Ho Chi Minh Trail, and as we worked our way north, we came upon several villages that I had never seen before. These villages were newly built, and all we could think of was that these villages were set up for all those NVA regiments that were heading south from the north.

One thing I never could figure out was sometimes we would be humping along, and all of a sudden we would see these young Vietnamese kids, about ten to twelve years old, and these kids would

try to sell us stuff, like a can of Coca-Cola. Where in hell, in the middle of this godforsaken place, did these kids get a can of Coke? This place was crazy, and nothing made sense at all.

Like I said, we would walk into these villages and papasan would meet us. We would search the village for any signs of NVA or any weapons, food, medical supplies, or whatever. Some of our men would get very upset, and tempers were very short. We had to remind them that we were the good guys, and that not everyone we encountered was the enemy. We would also see mamasan, and they all had black teeth from chewing betel nut. They chewed this betel nut because it made their gums numb. We also had kids trying to pimp their sisters. Yes, these kids would come up to you and say things like, "You like my sister, she number one, you like boom boom? She love you long time." Being a squad leader, I had to tell all my men to just keep walking and not to pay any attention to these kids. Well, babysan would be standing there, showing off her stuff, and it was hard to keep these marines focused on what we were there to do. I would tell the kids that they were number 10 and to *di-di*. Most often, we would find some type of contraband, and we would destroy the villages. Now remember, we had a large contingency of NVA regulars that were either on their way or already in these lowlands.

At night, we would set up our 360 perimeter, clear our field of fire, and set out our claymore mines and trip flares. Let me tell you one thing right now. I did not get much sleep while I was in 'Nam. You would hear all these horror stories about marines falling asleep at night while in their foxholes, and Charlie would sneak up and cut their throats. Well, not me. He's not going to get the chance to cut my throat. I would catch a catnap during the day whenever the battalion

would stop to rest. I knew that the nights belonged to the NVA, and you mostly stayed up all night just waiting for Charlie to attack your position. Hell, with that sapper company in our area, you didn't want to take a chance on catching any *z*'s.

During this one particular night, a couple of our trip flares went off in front of our lines. We figured that it was a squad from the NVA sapper unit, and we could see a couple of NVA regulars running. We opened fire, and when the rest of the company heard us open fire, the entire perimeter opened fire. Shit, no one had any idea what the hell they were shooting at, but there sure was a lot of lead flying out into the brush. Those red tracer rounds were everywhere. The Old Man got on the horn (radio) and asked what the hell was going on. I told him about the trip flares going off and that we observed a few NVA regulars running off, so the Old Man ordered that we saturate the area in front of our position with air support. We called in the big guns, and they fired on the area with their artillery. I loved it when these guys would send up artillery illumination rounds. It would light up the area just like daylight, and you could see very well. Anyway, as morning came, the Old Man had us go out and recon the area. We could see blood and drag marks where the NVA must have dragged their wounded and/or dead away. We later learned that we did get hit by about fifty or sixty sappers, but that the artillery did a number on them.

We continued to hump north, and we would catch a few skirmishes with the enemy, but nothing too serious. However, there were numerous contacts and sightings throughout the end of the month and into the first week of June. The Old Man felt that the enemy appeared to anticipate our operational maneuvers quite accurately, and he felt that we were being closely observed in this particular area of the operation. On the ninth of June, we finally arrived at Con Thien and got resupplied. I knew that things were going to start to get really interesting in a hurry. The Hill of Angels will never be the same again.

Con Thien was on high alert. We were advised that the NVA was continuously firing rockets and mortars upon the base almost every other hour. I noticed that we had twice the amount of Dusters and heavy artillery around our perimeter than we had before. It appeared to me that our intelligence officers knew more than what they informed us and that we were in for a real good time. The NVA seemed to be well-armed and supplied and ready to attack our positions at any time. In other words, the shit was going to hit the fan.

We sent out day and night patrols and saw all kinds of evidence that the NVA was certainly in the area. We uncovered several new bunker complexes and located AK-47 rounds and magazines, sixty and eighty-two-millimeter mortar rounds, Chicom grenades, bags of rice, wire cutters, three blocks of TNT, NVA ponchos, and miscellaneous papers.

On June 12, the NVA fired two 122-mm rockets at our perimeter. The old man ordered that we not fire back because he felt that it was a ploy by the NVA to try and see how fortified we were in that area. Instead, we called in artillery, and they saturated the area with artillery rounds. Then we had the choppers fly in, and they too opened up and sprayed the area with their fifty-caliber guns. That same night, as we did with every other night, we sent out a four-man LP (listening post), and they could observe the NVA trying to infiltrate the base. Again, artillery was called in, and the entire perimeter of the base was lit up. This lasted throughout the night, and the NVA never did penetrate our defensive positions.

The next morning, one of our trucks ran over a mine during a road sweep in front of the main gate. Four more mines were found, and one of our personnel carriers was disabled by another mine. Four marines were wounded and eventually medevaced out. Then we had these two Vietnamese women walk up to the perimeter of the main gate. They were ordered to stop, but they kept walking. Finally, the fire team guarding the gate received permission to fire warning shots, and these two women still kept coming. The women reached the outer wire, and again, they were ordered to stop and to turn around, but they kept coming. Finally, the Old Man gave the order to take them out, and that is exactly what happened. They were shot and killed before they could reach the inner wire of the gate.

These two women were then searched, and they had satchel charges strapped to their backs. Obviously, they were sent by the NVA on a suicide mission.

This is what occurred almost every day during the month of June. We went out on reinforced squad-size patrols, set up L-shape ambushes, and searched for the enemy. Several contacts were made, and we uncovered all kinds of enemy bunker complexes. We would get into small-arms firefights with the NVA, and they always retreated. We had several sightings of the NVA, and we called in artillery fire to attempt to block their escape routes to the north. Again, we also had several reports of friendly fire wounding and killing marines. These were so needless and careless. One marine was shot in the head by another marine during a smoke break. Another marine was hit in the back during an air strike. The bomb landed too close, and the marine got hit. This kind of shit appeared to happen all too often. It made you wonder if these guys running this crazy war really knew what in hell they were doing.

July came, and things didn't get any better. The heat was unbearable. We had more heat strokes than ever before. Marines were dropping like flies. We humped out of Con Thien and were replaced by an army division. Before leaving, we were all at the base together and were debriefing our replacements, when a soldier walked right into a minefield. We told them that the area was loaded with mines, but this idiot still walked out into the field and got blown up. What a waste!

We humped south and learned that Operation Virginia Ridge was coming to an end. They humped us into an area called the Denial Zone. Now, what in hell were we doing here? I mean, it was bad enough that the United States sprayed Agent Orange all over the I Corps area, which by the way was where we were operating. Now we were in an area called Denial Zone, which was an area west of Route 9, where CS gas was used to impede movement of the NVA into the area. They used that gas to keep the NVA out, but it was all right that we were operating in that area. Makes a lot of sense, doesn't it?

Now we had another operation, which took over Virginia Ridge, and that was Operation Idaho Canyon, which was in the same general area. Our operation orders were the same, and we used the same tactics of using squad—and platoon-size patrols in search-and-destroy missions. It became more and more evident that the NVA was everywhere. They infiltrated from the north, and they worked their way south. It was our job to find them, fight them, and stop them.

I was coming up on my turn to take R&R (rest and recreation), and I put in for a trip to either Bangkok and/or Singapore. The next thing I heard was that the Old Man denied my R&R request because he felt that he needed every marine in the bush. So needless to say, my R&R request was postponed! Great! So I stayed in the bush with my squad. I really didn't care anyway because I just figured it was that Murphy's law thing again. It became a real joke.

During one of our patrols, we came upon fresh footprints on the path. We followed these footprints. They led us to a large NVA trench living quarters. We found miscellaneous cooking utensils, rifle racks, sleeping quarters, bandages, first-aid supplies, water, rice, ammunition, AK-47 magazines, and a lot of paperwork. There was a tunnel leading to an underground-type hospital. Needless to say, we blew the place all to hell. The Old Man was really happy with himself at first, and then at the same time, he was upset because we did not find any NVA soldiers. Of course he was upset—no freaking body count. Speaking of body counts, I loved that term. How in hell could anyone in their right mind ever think that they were getting an accurate body count out here in this mess of a place? First off, we hardly ever saw any dead bodies. Sure, we saw signs of the enemy, like blood trails, bloody bandages, sneakers, or sandals, but hardly ever any dead bodies. We would get into a firefight, and command would estimate a body count without any bodies. The only time that I saw a real body count was when we would get into the shits, and we would have these NVA bodies actually dead right in front of us. Now that was a real body count and not some speculation of how many NVA we killed.

By now, we were in the bush for quite a while, and we were all getting pretty ripe. Our uniforms were so dirty and old looking that many of us had rips and holes in our jungle fatigues, and our crotches were starting to rot out. I remember once I needed a bath so badly that I noticed a large bomb crater that was full of water. Not thinking at all of what might be in that water, I just took off my gear and jumped in that bomb crater. A few minutes later, a couple of my guys jumped

in too. Now, just think of this, there could have been water snakes or whatever else in that water, but we didn't care. We just needed to get in that water to try and cool off and try and clean ourselves up. Luckily, nothing happened, and we just went in that crater filled with muddy water and came out. No one said a freaking word, no one. A few of us even filled up our empty canteens with that water, and then we loaded these canteens with halogen pills and presweetened Kool-Aid to kill the taste. Yes, life was a real thrill in the bush. We had marines who got malaria, diarrhea, heat exhaustion, foot diseases like trench foot, and sanitation infections. Hell, if it wasn't one thing, it was another.

We kept humping from one hill to another, and at night, we would set up our perimeter around the hill. Then we would set up an LZ (landing zone) for the choppers to fly in and resupply us. At night we sent out our night ambush patrols and listening post. One morning, while we were on our ambush patrol along a dried streambed, we came face-to-face with about forty NVA. These gooks were dressed in green uniforms, not camouflaged, and carrying packs and weapons. We opened fire, and they dropped their packs and ran off. We continued to fire and called in artillery. We searched the area, and we could not find one of these NVA soldiers. We searched their packs, and they were packed with wire crimpers, time fuses, blasting caps, and several small blocks of C-3, which was like dynamite.

During the end of the month, it became very evident that the NVA was building up in our area. Instead of seeing small groups of NVA we were now seeing platoon-size groups and larger. Charlie was definitely on the move. We received word from one of our artillery observers that a company of NVA, approximately two hundred, were moving east in our direction. The Old Man ordered that we dig in and dig in good. We were just west of Cam Lo, and we had been in this area before. Now we were digging in, again, for what could be a real good fight.

We set up our perimeter and were dug in good. As night came, we could hear noises coming from the bush, and we all knew that it was Charlie coming our way. It was like they wanted us to hear them coming. They wanted to psych us out. Hell, they even carried torches as they climbed up our hill toward our position. Of all the places that the NVA could hit us, it was right on our platoon's lines, Second Platoon's line got probed by an NVA sapper platoon, and vicious grenades, rocket-launchers, and small-arms battle ensued. They hit us with everything they had and finally broke through our defensive lines. Now the worst and most deadly thing that could ever happen did—we had gooks inside our perimeter. Red and green tracers were flying everywhere. One of my marines, in a foxhole next to me, was yelling and screaming. He needed help. I crawled over to his hole, and another marine was trying to help him and calm him down. I told that marine to keep firing at the gooks as they were coming right at us. I looked at this wounded marine and realized that it was Denny, a good friend of mine, and I gave him a couple of shots of morphine. You see, we carried our morphine shots, which were what we called slap shots. Denny was hurt badly, as an RPG had gone off right in front of him. His face was full of blood, and I could not see his eyes. It appeared that the top of his head had been torn off. I never saw so much fucking blood in my life. I kept calling for a corpsman. No one came. I tried to stop the bleeding, and I bandaged up his face as best I could. At the same time, I was firing my weapon at anything that moved in front or on the sides of me. As the morphine kicked in, Denny started to quiet down, and he asked me not to let him die. I assured him that he wasn't going to die on my fucking watch. I laid him down in his foxhole and told him that I would be back to get him. I told his partner to watch over him and not to let the NVA reach their foxhole. I gave that marine extra grenades that I had, and I moved on to another foxhole. As I was crawling, I remember seeing the Old Man, Captain Dan, and our lieutenant out in the open, on their stomachs, giving out orders—"Get these bastards," "Shoot these sons of bitches," "Don't let them get inside our perimeter." All kinds of shit was being said. The Old Man was up and down like a goddamn kangaroo. Our lieutenant and his radioman tried to follow him, but Dan was so quick. All I know is that these bastards kept coming and it didn't seem to end. Lead was flying around all over the place. Hand grenades were being thrown everywhere, and bodies were mounting up. It seems that the fighting was going on forever and would never stop. We had gunships in the area working out with their fifty-caliber guns. We had Puff working out with his guns. We had artillery called in, and it felt like the whole hill was going to be flattened. All we could do was keep firing at these crazy, slant-eyed bastards as they kept coming up into our lines. It was chaos and mayhem, and my ears were ringing so loudly because of all the explosions. Marines were yelling and screaming all over the place. I was never so fucking scared in my life but I knew that I had to keep going. That I couldn't let this fear that I felt inside get the best of me. I crawled over to another marine. He was crying so loudly and kept saying, "Please help me, don't leave me alone." I again called for a corpsman, and again, no one came. I looked at this marine who was attached to First Squad. His guts were all over the ground next to him. He was bleeding really badly, and all I could see were his guts on the ground. I grabbed another marine and told him to give this wounded marine a slap shot, which he did. I grabbed a handful of his guts and tried to shove them back into his stomach. I tried so hard, and then I used his first-aid bandages and mine to keep his guts from spilling out. He kept on crying, and I told the other marine to give him another slap shot. We pulled that marine into a foxhole and told him to just stay there and keep putting pressure on his stomach and not to let the bandages fall off and that he would get medevaced soon. He kept saying, "Please do not let me die alone." I assured him that he wasn't going to die and that he would get out of here as soon as one of our birds could land. Our medevac choppers were trying to land, but the gooks kept firing their RPG rockets at them so they couldn't land. Without a doubt, this was the worse firefight that I had ever been in, and I thought to myself, *When is all of this shit going to end?* I kept firing and throwing grenades, and my M-79 man was firing that thing as fast as he could. I grabbed the M-79 from him, and I shot that thing, point-blank range, at several gooks. Mortar platoon was firing their mortars so close to us that it wasn't funny. The shit really hit the fan, and this time, no one knew if they were going to die or survive this attack. All I know was that I wasn't going to let these bastards get me. I fought with everything I had. I kept yelling to my men not to let these motherfuckers get into our lines. "Kill these bastards, don't let them in!"

The fighting continued until dawn, and when it all stopped—I never thought that it would—we had bodies everywhere. We lost our lieutenant, the Old Man, Captain Dan, and his radioman. We had so many marines who were wounded. We tried to regain our strength and composure and get all our wounded and dead to the LZ to be medevaced out. I learned that the head corpsman was also a casualty of this firefight, and that was the reason, when I called for a corpsman, no one came. I walked over to the foxhole that my buddy, Denny, was in, and he was still alive. I carried him to the LZ and laid him down on a poncho liner and told him that the choppers were here and he'd be out of here soon. He thanked me for all I did, and I had tears coming down my face. Good thing he couldn't see me crying. He always thought that I was a tough marine, and he wished that he could have been tough like me. Well, to be totally honest, I wasn't tough at all, and I felt all his pain. I thought to myself, *What a fucking shame, these are supposed to be the best years of our life, right! I am in the prime of my life, twenty years old, what a fucking joke! We are here to fight against Communism and to give these slant-eyed bastards freedom.* Murphy's law—if it's going to happen, it will. Man, what a fucking night. My ears were still ringing, and I could just barely hear. What was I doing here? I wasn't drafted; I enlisted for this shit. To fight for someone's freedom, and they really don't care about their freedom at all. What a shame that our men—boys—were dying for these people who could care less. Well, this time, we had that fucking body count that they talked about. We had dead gooks everywhere. The fighting may have stopped, but we all had to live with what happened here for the rest of our lives. We were the lucky ones. We survived this night. Actually, how lucky were we, really? This is something that will haunt each and every one of us forever.

I checked on each one of my men, and we tried our best to get back to setting up our perimeter to safeguard the rest of the platoon. We checked our ammunition and searched the dead NVA. We sent out small patrols, in the event that any more NVA solders were out in the bush in front of us. We found a lot of blood trails, and we knew that we survived this fight by the grace of God. It just wasn't our time to go. God had spared us to live another day in 'Nam. I walked over to First Squad's position and noticed that the marine who we placed in the foxhole was not there. I thought to myself, *I only hope that he made it and that he was still alive, that someone carried this marine to the medevac area.* Once everyone was medevaced out, choppers came in and resupplied us with more ammunition, food, water, and replacements. We stayed in the bush and continued with the operation, Idaho Canyon, which was not yet over for us, and we humped and continued with the search-and-destroy missions.

During this time, we continued to have several sightings of the NVA, and we knew that these bastards were here to stay. They wanted their country back, and it was evident that they were going to do whatever it took to get it. This was the beginning of what was to come. The NVA was here to stay, and that was becoming clear as each day passed by. They were becoming stronger and more tenacious and aggressive in their tactics. This war was far from being over, and it was becoming clear to me that we really did not belong here.

In mid-September, we were airlifted from the bush and were flown to Vandegrift Combat Base. We were ordered to stand down and were eventually transported, by truck convoy, to Quang Tri. During this trip to Quang Tri, we had a security aerial observer overhead as an escort as we traveled back south. Our combat role in Vietnam had come to an end for the marines of First Battalion, Third Marine Division, and I was going to be reassigned to another marine unit, south of Da Nang. At the end of September 1969, I was reassigned to F Company, Second Battalion, First Marine Division (Fox 2/1).

CHAPTER 7

Fox 2/1

I arrived by convoy at Cau Ha Combat Base, which was the home of Second Battalion. This combat base was located in Quang Nan Province, just southwest of Da Nang. I noted that the terrain leading to the base was flat and sandy, with rice paddies and broken tree lines. There were several villages leading to the base, and the cover and concealment around the base was fair, and observation was very good. I thought to myself that this was a walk in the park because there were no mountains to climb like there were in Quang Tri Province. I unloaded my gear and was escorted to the base commander. After a quick debriefing of where I had previously been assigned, he placed me into Fox Company of 2/1. I met with the company commander, and he also debriefed me as to what my combat experience consisted of while in Bravo 1/3. After our debriefing, he advised that with my combat experience, he was going to have me meet up with the platoon sergeant, and while doing so, he advised that I would be a prime candidate to become a squad leader. The platoon sergeant advised that as far as he was concerned, I should be promoted to corporal very soon so that I could take over one of his squads.

Now let me tell you, these marines here had it pretty good. They had a chow hall and ate hot meals. They had hot showers, and they were all assigned sleeping quarters, with cots and blankets and footlockers for your gear. When they went out on patrol, they didn't have to carry any heavy packs because they always came back to the base at the end of their patrol. Sure, they did have to take shifts at perimeter guard duty, but everyone shared in taking shifts. God, I might even be able to have a night's sleep. What a thought.

We would go out on patrols, mostly on search-and-destroy missions, looking for any VC or, in rare cases, NVA soldiers. The villages were constantly under surveillance, and we searched them almost every day. We did have night patrols, but it was nothing like I was used to up north. Mostly, we were fighting small numbers of the NVA, and it was like guerilla warfare. It was more like terrorist attacks, because the VC would raid the villages at night and they would assassinate anyone who appeared to be sympathetic to our cause.

After a couple of weeks, I got promoted to corporal, and I did take over a squad. This was the same squad that I was assigned to when I first arrived. I knew all of the men in the squad and I knew who I could count on and who were the slackers. Every squad had their slackers. These were the marines who just didn't care about anything and all they did was just enough to get by and stay out of trouble. They liked to smoke weed and just skate under the radar of any NCO (noncommissioned officer) who was in charge of them. I knew who they were and I had that advantage. Everything seemed to be going great. Like I said, we would go on patrol almost every day and we would also be tasked with security duty for the mine sweeping teams. Every morning, we would have these mine sweeping teams go out onto the main road leading to our base and all they did was use mine sweeping equipment, metal detectors, and they would make sure that the road was free and clear from any land mines that the VC or the NVA placed in the road during the previous night. So every squad took turns acting as their security as they swept the road. The only concern that I had was the occasional nuisance RPG incoming or a lob grenade by the enemy, which went on almost every night. You would never know if one of these rounds would have your name on it, so you had to be diligent and aware of what was going on around you.

CHAPTER 8

Taps

Then I had an idea. I wrote a letter home and asked a friend of mine if he would be able to send me a bugle from the drum corps. The next thing I knew, after about three weeks, I received a care package and a bugle from the corps. Let me tell you, did I ever open up a whole new can of worms for myself. This combat base had a United States and a Marine Corps flag flying every day. So one evening, just about dusk, I walked outside of my barracks, stood at attention, and sounded taps on that bugle. That echoed all over the base, and anyone who was

outside, just stopped in their tracks and listened to the sound of taps. Now, unbeknownst to me, the battalion sergeant major was walking from the mess hall, and when he heard taps being played, he stopped, faced the flag, and saluted until taps was done. Then all shit hit the fan. The hunt was on for whoever played taps. The sergeant major approached the base commander, and they all wanted to know who the hell played taps. The only marines who knew it was me were the marines in my squad. The platoon sergeant finally came to our hooch and inquired if anyone heard taps being played. The gig was up, and I told him that I was the one who played taps, and I apologized if I caused any problems. The next thing I knew, I was standing tall before the base commander and the sergeant major. At first, I thought that I was in the shits, but the commander wanted to know where I got the horn and where and when did I learn how to play taps. I explained that I had been playing a bugle ever since I was eight years old and that I was part of a drum and bugle corps for ten years back in the World. He told me that it has been a long time since he has heard such a sweet-sounding sound of those twenty-four notes of taps. To make a long story short, both the sergeant major and the commander asked me if I would play taps every night. I told them that I would be proud and it would be my honor to play taps on this base. I thanked them. From that moment on, both the commander and the sergeant major would always make it a point to talk with me, and every night, they both stood outside and saluted as I played taps. I couldn't do any wrong now. The sergeant major would take me aside and would always talk to me about what sounding taps did for morale of the troops. I often had men in my squad ask me what the meaning of taps was. I said to them there are no official words to the music. It was written a long time ago, and those twenty-four notes have many meanings, but the most popular verse is "Day is done. Gone the sun, from the lakes, from the hills, from the sky. All is well. Safely rest. God is nigh." Imagine, here I was in the middle of Vietnam on some godforsaken firebase, with the gooks and the Viet Cong all around us, and here I was playing taps. A battalion sergeant major was like God. Whatever he said was gospel, and no one ever questioned him, not even the commanding officer. Once he told me that if I ever needed anything or if anyone ever gave me any shit or a hard time, to just let him know and he would take care of it himself. I continued to play taps every day, and if anyone was seen walking around while I played taps, there was hell to pay.

One afternoon while I was running a sandbag detail, the sergeant major walked over to me, and we started talking about all kinds of things. He eventually asked me when the last time was that I was on R&R. I told him that I had not been on R&R ever since I got into this country, back in March. The next thing I knew, I was issued a jeep, and he told me to take a few days and to go into Da Nang. I explained that my best friend was somewhere in 'Nam and that it would be great if I could meet up with him while I was in Da Nang. He asked me his name and then walked off. A couple of hours later, he had located where this marine was and arranged for me to meet him in Da Nang. This friend and I grew up together, and we both joined the marine corps together. Remember that boot marine who had his knee broken while in boot camp at Parris Island? This was that marine, and I hadn't seen or heard from him ever since he went into the infirmary for his broken knee. The sergeant major told me about a friend of his who was a warrant officer, that this friend was the commander of the drum and bugle corps, which was stationed at the First and Third Marine Division, just outside of Da Nang at Camp Horn. He said that he reached out to that warrant officer and told him about me playing taps, that I had a sweet sound as I played. Sergeant major also arranged for me to audition for a position in the drum and bugle corps.

I drove the jeep to Da Nang and everything was prearranged for my billeting. I arrived at the Third Marine Corps Amphibious Force (III MAF) at Camp Horn. I eventually auditioned for the drum and bugle corps and was offered a position as a first soprano bugler. Man, was I walking on air! Never in my entire life did I expect this to happen to me. I dreamed about playing my horn in the Marine Corps, but I really never thought it would come true. Hell, I cannot even read music, but they didn't know that, and I aced that freaking audition. I was told to think about the offer and let my sergeant major know what my decision was. I drove over to the main PX (exchange) in Da Nang and met with my friend. We spent the rest of the day together, drinking beer at the NCO club. I just couldn't believe my good fortune. After two days, I drove back to Cau Ha Combat Base.

Things seemed to keep getting better for me. One morning, the commanding officer sent for me, and when I walked into his office, the sergeant major was also there. I was told that I was going to be sent back home to the World for my R&R. God, I couldn't believe it. Was I dreaming or was this actually happening? The sergeant major made all the arrangements for me to take a thirty—(30) day leave back to the World. I was going to be home for Christmas. I never told anyone back home that I was coming home for Christmas.

CHAPTER 9

R&R to the World

I left Da Nang airport on a C-130 and landed in Okinawa. I had a layover in Okinawa and then got on a commercial airline, Tiger Airlines and, eventually, two days later, landed in Los Angeles. When I got off the plane and walked into the terminal, I was surrounded by all these damn war demonstrators. I was in my marine uniform, and these assos were calling me all kinds of names. One girl spit on my uniform and called me a baby killer. I wanted to just reach out and knock her on her ass. Instead, I just kept walking through the terminal to catch a connecting flight to Boston. What I didn't know was that the Marine Corps, in all their wisdom, paid my father a visit. I guess it was quite a sight seeing that official Marine Corps vehicle pull up to my parents' home. Right away, my parents thought that something bad had happened to me and that they were there to inform them. Two (2) marines, dressed in their dress blue uniform, asked if they could talk with my dad. My dad calmed my mom down and told her that they only wanted to tell them that I was well, and they wanted to explain what to expect when I got home. My dad was the only one who knew that I would be home for Christmas. These marines told my dad that I was not the same boy who left a year ago and that they just wanted to reach out and advise him that I may have nightmares and may act a little strange because of what I experienced while in Vietnam and that Dad should think about where he was going to have me stay while at home. So the old man, in all his great wisdom, made a bedroom down in our basement.

I landed in Boston and then took a bus to our hometown. Once in town, I took a cab home. I walked into the house two (2) days before Christmas. I thought that my mom was going to faint right there. She was so shocked to see me. All she did was start crying and grab me and hug me so tight. Mom kept repeating that she could not believe that I was home. She was real happy and very emotional. After a while, Dad walked me downstairs and told me that he made me a special place to stay while I was home and that I was going to be sleeping in the basement. Shit, you know, it was just like staying in a bunker. What the hell was this? Anyway, I didn't want to cause any problems, so I didn't say a word.

My girlfriend didn't even know I was home. I asked if I could use the car to drive over to her home in the next town. Dad gave me the keys to his car, and I drove to her house. I thought that she was going to have a heart attack. She couldn't believe that no one told her I was coming home. She was crying and would not stop hugging me. Anyway, everything worked out in the end. She had my car, so she followed me back home, and I drove her back home in my car. While I was home, I mostly stayed at her house anyway. The holidays went very well, and I didn't spaz out, except for one morning. My mom came downstairs to wake me up, and as she reached me, I jumped up and almost punched her in the face. Mom never came downstairs again. I really scared her, and you know, I really scared myself.

After Christmas, I went to the credit union to get some of my money, which I was having sent home each month. I learned that I only had a couple hundred dollars in my account. I said that was impossible because I was sending almost all my money home for over a year now. I was told that my dad had taken out most of my money some time ago. I couldn't believe it. Why would he take my freaking money? It wasn't his, and God knows that I earned that money. I would never earn money like that again. I was in a war, and I earned that money shooting and killing gooks. What the hell was he thinking anyway? I questioned him on why he took my money, and I was told that he needed it for my sister's wedding. I asked him, "What the hell, you used my money without asking me so that you could pay for a wedding that I wasn't even at?" Man, was I pissed. I approached my mom and asked her if she knew that Dad had taken my money out of my account and used it to pay for the wedding. All my mom said was that my father didn't know where he was going to get the money to pay for my sister's wedding, so he figured I wouldn't mind if he used my money. I tried to explain to my mom that Dad had no right to take my money without my permission. Mom only said, "You know your father, and he figured it was all right." It was only a loan, and that someday, he would pay me back. Man, he'd pay me back all right, when hell freezes over. I just got into my car and drove to my girlfriend's house. From that day on,

I never sent a cent back home again. I changed all my paperwork and had my money—my monthly pay—sent to my girl. She made sure that the money went into another account that I had opened under both my name and her name. Good old Dad, I knew that he would never let me down and that he would never use me again. It wasn't bad enough that I was staying in the damn basement; now I learned that he also took my freaking money. Figures! Nothing was ever easy at home. Nothing made any sense at all. Shit, I couldn't wait to get back to 'Nam. At least, while I was in 'Nam, I knew exactly what to expect. Being home was just a chore, and I had to put up with his crazy shit again. I only hope that everyone had a good time at the wedding—on my dime.

I made up my mind that I was going to extend my tour in 'Nam and that I was also going to take the warrant officer's offer up on being transferred to the marine drum and bugle corps. I didn't tell anyone, including my girl, of my decision because I didn't need to hear her shit about extending. I figured that once I got back, I would write to her and tell her.

It finally came time for me to leave the World again and start heading back to 'Nam. I asked my dad if he would take me to Boston so that I could get my flight out to LA. He hemmed and hawed, and finally he said he would. Again, Dad didn't let me down and made it clear that he was going out of his way to give me that ride. We all packed up, my mom and my girl, and Dad drove me into Boston. Once at the airport, he had a hard time finding a place to park. Here we go again. It was everybody's fault that he couldn't find a parking place. He was swearing and said that it figured, because he was trying to do me a favor, but it backfired because he couldn't park anywhere near the terminal. I told him to just stop the car and drop me off, but my mom told him to keep looking for a parking place. He finally found an open space, and after parking, we had to walk quite a ways to the terminal. Yes, you guessed it, it was my freaking fault that he parked so far away. We finally reached the terminal, and my flight was postponed for an hour. Again, that was my fault too. Shit, it was always my fault when shit like this happened. Finally, it was time for me to depart. My mom was crying, and she gave me a big hug and a kiss and told me to take care of myself. My girl was also crying and told me that she loved me and that she was going to miss me and to please write as soon as I can. Dad never shook my hand, never hugged me or said a word. He just watched me as I walked toward the flight gate. Man, I really could not wait to get the hell out of there.

I boarded the plane and flew to Los Angeles. Once in Los Angeles, I again was yelled at and called names by these damn war demonstrators. God, didn't these assos have anything better to do with their lives? What a bunch of losers! You would think that the police or airport security would be all over these nuts, but they weren't. They just let them harass all the uniformed service men and women who were coming in and/or going out of the airport.

A few days later, I landed back in Okinawa and stayed in Oki overnight. I grabbed a hop on a C-130 that was heading back into Da Nang, and I finally landed at the Da Nang airport. I made my way over to III MAF headquarters at Camp Horn and met with the commander of the drum and bugle corps. I told him that I wanted to extend my tour of duty and that I would be honored to be transferred into the drum and bugle corps. He advised that he would start the necessary paperwork for the transfer and that it should take about two weeks to get everything completed. He had one of his sergeants give me a ride back to Cau Ha combat base.

Once back at the base, I met with my commanding officer and the sergeant major and advised them of my plans. They both agreed that this was the best plan for me. While I waited for my orders to come in, I went back to my squad. Like before, every evening I again played taps until the day my orders finally came. I packed up all my gear, said

all my good-byes, and told the sergeant major how much I appreciated all his assistance. All he said to me was good luck. That I already did my time in the bush and now it was time that the Marine Corps did something for me. I thanked God for giving me a break and for giving me the opportunity to fulfill my dream of playing in the Marine Corps drum and bugle corps, which is also known as the Commandant's Own.

CHAPTER 10

Marine Drum and Bugle Corps

I was transported to Camp Horn and was immediately introduced to the other members of the drum corps. I was assigned to share a room with the company clerk. He was a real good guy, and we became close friends. I practiced with the corps, learned their repertoire, and I was playing first soprano within the week. Then I got another surprise. I was promoted to sergeant. Man, I couldn't believe my good fortune. I was in the Marine Corps for less than two years now and I was already promoted to Sergeant, E-5. Things were happening fast, and I really enjoyed playing that horn again. It didn't take long that I became one of the soloists. What an honor, and I felt so good.

Now don't get me wrong, it wasn't all peaches and cream. We played and practiced during the day, and at night, we were part of a special security company. You see, being attached to command, we were the night security for what was known as Hill 327, which was also known as Freedom Hill, and this hill surrounded the northern perimeter of Da Nang. Let me tell you what great duty I had. Because of my 0311 training and combat experience, I was the NCO in charge of security. I had a jeep, and all I did was drive along the roadway of Hill 327 and made sure that each bunker complex was well manned and that they were all on alert. We didn't have to pull security duty every night. We shared the responsibility of security with all the other divisions that were attached to III MAF, so we would stand security about once a week. Not bad!

During the day, when we were not practicing, we performed music concerts and what they called troop and stomp events for change-of-command ceremonies and award ceremonies, and we played gigs at Marble Mountain, Monkey Mountain, and China Beach, which was always a treat, because after our concert, we would spend the remainder of the day swimming in the China Sea. We played for all the dignitaries who came into the Da Nang area, and we also played at dedications and performed concerts for the troops and in the villages surrounding the Da Nang area. Hell, we played for anybody and everybody who would listen to us. I never figured that I would have a chance like this, ever, in my lifetime. During our marching gigs, the Vietnamese kids gathered and loved to watch us march by while we played our horns. I was finally in my element!

In mid-August of 1970, the commander called me into his quarters and advised that I was going to be redeployed back to the World. In other words, I was going home. He advised that I was one hell of an exceptional musician and that I was a natural horn player, and he asked if I wanted to continue playing once I got back to the States. He further stated that if I did, I would be promoted to staff sergeant (E-6) and would be attached to headquarters battalion in Washington, DC. I would be part of the Commandant's Own Drum and Bugle Corps at Eighth and I. Now let me tell you, this was it. The Commandant's Own was the best of the best in the drum corps world. It was such an honor to be asked to be a part of this prestigious and world-renowned group. Now let me explain what this meant. I would be transferred to headquarters battalion, marine barracks in Washington, DC, which is located at the corner of Eighth and I Streets, hence the name Eighth and I. This duty station is the oldest post in the United States Marine Corps and is the official residence of the commandant of the Marine Corps. It is, without a doubt, the most prestigious duty station a marine could ever be assigned to. I advised that I would have to think about this offer, and I thanked him for such an honor. He advised me that he had to write up a fitness report and that I had to sign off on his report. This is what he wrote in his remarks:

> Sgt. Duchesneau is a talented musician demonstrating above average skills as a bugler. With his past "03" experience, he has been invaluable as a line NCO on the perimeter security. He has great potential as a Marine Bandsman. He is military competent and seeks responsibility. He most assuredly possesses the requisite skills in his new MOS (5591) for advancement to the next higher grade. This report covers the period in a combat zone.

This was written and signed by the commander of the Marine Corps drum and bugle corps, warrant officer IV on August 11, 1970.

I wrote back home to my girl and told her about the offer. I told her that this was quite an honor and that I was extremely proud to be selected for this assignment. She flatly advised that if I stayed in the Marine Corps and continued playing in their drum and bugle corps, she was not going to wait for me any longer. All she wanted was for me to come home so that we could get married. Of course she did. Do you think that maybe she would think about what I wanted to do with my life? Hell no! Anyway, I was honored to have been asked, and I left it at that. I was eventually transferred out of Vietnam and traveled back to Okinawa and was given the opportunity to receive an early out of the Marine Corps. All my paperwork was processed, and within two weeks, I was transferred into the inactive United States Marine Corps Reserves with an honorable discharge. I arrived back in the World. I was on my way back home. My Marine Corps days were over, and I can honestly say, I will never, ever, regret joining the Marine Corps and being able to live the life and experience of a grunt in the northern part of Vietnam, near and around the DMZ with Bravo 1/3 and then being redeployed south to Fox 2/1 and having the great opportunity of being a part of the greatest drum and bugle corps in the world, the United States Marine Drum & Bugle Corps! You know, they say, "What goes around comes around." I think I now know how my dad felt about wondering how his life would have turned out if only he went to college. Well, I always wondered how my life would have turned out if I had stayed in the Marine Corps drum and bugle corps and followed my dreams. I guess only God will know. All I can say is that God watched over me and blessed me during this part of my life, which, as they say, will live on in infinity.

When I arrived back in the World, like before when I was home on leave, I proudly wore my Marine Corps uniform for the last time, and again, like before, there were all these protesters. We had no ceremonies, no parades, no greeters welcoming me home—nothing.

All I can say is that I proudly did my duty for the corps and my country. I never asked for anything in return other than to be respected for doing my duty.

The End